W9-CES-791

Other People's Property

Other People's Property

Bernard H. Siegan

Published in Cooperation with
the University of San Diego

Lexington Books
D.C. Heath and Company
Lexington, Massachusetts
Toronto   London

Library of Congress Cataloguing in Publication Data
Siegan, Bernard H.
    Other people's property. *See slip*

~~Includes index.~~
    1. Zoning—United States. 2. Land—United States.
I. Title.
HD260.S53   333.3'0973   75-22884
ISBN 0-669-00187-2

Copyright © 1976 by Bernard H. Siegan

Published simultaneously in Canada

Printed in the United States of America

International Standard Book Number: 0-669-00187-2

Library of Congress Catalog Card Number: 75-22884

To Sharon

Contents

Preface

Most of the ideas to be found in this book first appeared in whole or embryonic form in columns and articles I wrote for the Freedom newspapers, Santa Ana *Register, Colorado Springs Gazette-Telegraph, Baltimore Sun* and the *Environmental Law* journal. The focus of those articles and this book is on the use of the land, a subject that relates to a great many concerns of the day. These include: individual freedom, housing, employment, business, taxes, competition, environmental quality, growth, energy, food and conservation. Decisions on the use of land may have an impact on some or possibly all of these interests, either directly or indirectly.

Public land use decision-making also affects personal interests, and consequently is responsive to them. People differ greatly in their positions on and approaches to land use. For example, the growth of a community will be viewed in one perspective by those who already live in it and in another by those who would like to settle there. Environmentalists and developers will have vastly different opinions on the consequences of building on a site adjoining the ocean.

A major problem for organized society is how best to resolve controversies between competing interests and groups. In the case of land use, there are at least three broad possibilities. The government could completely control the decision-making process; it could share control with private industry; or it could allow the private sector largely free rein. The second alternative is descriptive of the zoning system under which most land use is regulated in this country.

Over the years, government's share of the decision-making process has been increasing substantially. The results have been far from satisfactory, and there is no reason to believe they will improve. It is my view that a different course should be taken. Government regulation of land use should be minimized, and we should rely instead largely on the restraints inherent in individual freedom and competition to control the use of land. The reasons for this conclusion are set forth in the pages that follow.

Bernard H. Siegan
La Jolla, California
October 20, 1975

ix

1 The Failure of Land Use Planning

Implicit in the push for national land use legislation is the notion that new or better urban planning can solve major problems of land use. In practice, however, public planning of land use is erratic, chaotic, and irrational; it produces many more problems than it solves. This is clearly the lesson of fifty years of zoning experience in the United States. Zoning like any other regulation of land use is supposed to be a tool of planning and, therefore, we can learn much from it about the operation of the planning process.

The Panacea of Planning

There is some appeal in the notion that we must have more and better planning. After all, goes the refrain, if we only had planned our cities better, there would be less congestion, no slums, more beautiful buildings, etc. There is always someone who can describe in exhausting detail a local horror that could have been avoided by better, stricter, sounder, some, or even any planning. On investigation, it frequently develops that the local planning department had approved that particular horror. The argument continues: do not individuals and corporations carefully plan their activities and outlays? Why then should government not be allowed or required to engage in this selfsame activity?

The simple, yet highly profound answer is that public land use planning is doomed to failure in a representative society.

Planning—Science, Art, or Politics?

Public land use planning means or implies an orderly, rational arrangement of or for the use of land for the present or the future, directed or controlled by detached experts in planning.

Although this definition raises many questions, it represents

1

what most people think they are saying when they speak or write of planning. The assumption seems to be that there is something precise, measurable, or quantitative about planning, or its standards; in other words, that it is, or is comparable to, a science.

This assumption is exceedingly difficult to substantiate and few of even its most ardent proponents make the effort. Is there some precise measurement available to determine the "best" use of some or all of the land, of growth and antigrowth proposals, of whether the land is better suited for trees, lagoons, or the housing of people? Should the land be developed with two, eight, or twelve housing units to the acre, or perhaps it is better suited for a mobile home park or a shopping center, or should it be retained as open space? By now, after fifty years of zoning experience in this country, it should be clear that there are respectable, distinguished, and knowledgeable planners who would disagree in many if not most instances to any or all of these alternatives. Planning is unquestionably highly subjective, lacking those standards and measurements that are requisites of a scientific discipline.

To settle any doubts on this score, simply read the record in most zoning cases. Typically, one finds testimony from two planners, one supporting the plaintiff (land owner), and the other favoring the defendant (city). At the trial level, many zoning cases have become verbal duels between planners, each promoting a substantially different position. Accordingly, what goes under the name of planning is an opinion by someone who has studied and is learned in the creation, growth, and development of cities. The country's zoning experience raises serious doubts that such training and knowledge provides any special insights, either in evaluating the present or in predicting the future.

Planners confront serious problems in fulfilling their responsibilities. Theory and education alone cannot substitute for the actual experience of making practical decisions and suffering their consequences. Few planners have ever been part of the construction or development industry, or responsible for actual decisions in the development of residential, commercial, or industrial projects. Even if they once had been, their information about prices, materials, innovations and trends, and consumer desires and preferences must necessarily now come from secondary or more remote sources, not directly from the "firing line." How then can planners possibly be as familiar with the development, construction, and operation of shopping centers, housing developments, nursing homes, or mobile parks as those who develop, own, and operate them? Owners and their mortgage lenders risk substantial funds on their success. Yet, planners are expected to regulate all of them, which is akin to asking the blind to lead those who can see. Unfortunately, for the community, in lieu of hard information, they will tend to rely on their own experience and background, and this inevitably creates hardships and problems for those of different perspectives, tastes, and attitudes.

But, regardless of their knowledge, training and abilities, the fact is that planners are not destined to make a significant impact on the regulation of land use. The decisions and controls will be adopted by politicians or those appointed by politicians. They can be expected to and will respond to a variety of pressures and concerns, a principal one being the interests of those who place them and keep them in office. Politics, rather than planning, will be largely involved. In short, zoning and other land use regulations are and have to be a tool more of politics than of planning.

Politics and Pressures

Consider these limitations on the power of the planner. First, he is a paid employee and cannot be expected to espouse with any degree of consistency policies contrary to those of his employers. The basic rules are established by those elected to govern or appointed to administer. Confrontations are probably rare because a planner is not likely to be hired or seek employment if his basic orientation appears to differ substantially from that of his prospective employers. Planners committed to growth could find life quite uncomfortable in the "no-growth" communities. The reverse is equally true. Disagreements will occur and be tolerated—within limitations.

Second, even if a proposed plan appears in accord with the general desires of the law makers or administrators, and its preparation may actually have been commissioned by them, there will still have to be public hearings and debates before it can be adopted. Amendments required for passage can easily change the meaning and impact of the proposed legislation. In practice, the "perfect" plan stands little chance of remaining intact against the opposition of a group of voters or politicians, the pressures exerted by political supporters or contributors, the payment of graft or perhaps even the voice of the local newspaper. Accordingly, the "perfect" plan is likely to be quite imperfect by the time it emerges from the legislative process, whether it be on a local or higher governmental level, and it miqht be ravaged still more as administered. It is possible that the courts ultimately may lay some or much of it to rest.

Nor is the plan or law that is finally passed likely to remain intact very long. From the moment of its adoption, special interest groups such as environmentalists, developers, and civic clubs, will seek to change it to their own benefit. It will never have enough open space for the many environmentalists hostile to development. Nor will those who can, by changing the regulations reap huge profits sit idly by.

They will make every conceivable effort to change the classification on their properties or those they would like to buy. They will attempt to increase the number of units per acre or change the category from residential to commercial or apartments to industrial, or vice-versa. Civic groups, likewise, will sooner or later find the plan wanting in some or many respects.

Many of these pressures are bound to succeed and that super plan will shortly have little more value than as a reference document for the historian. The changes will be made on a piecemeal basis and promiscuously, guided principally by political rather than planning considerations.

Some acknowledge the limitations of the public process, but contend this is the price society must pay to save our land. They say that because land is so unique and scarce, its use cannot be left to the vagaries of the marketplace. Such arguments ignore the strong controls inherent in a private economic system.

Obviously, there should be great concern that land is not wasted or spoiled. It is one of our most precious resources. That is why we should prefer the controls of the private rather than the political marketplace. For in the latter, expediency and incompetency will inevitably prevail.

Builders and developers, like all entrepreneurs, have to be reasonably expert at their business. They have to use the land efficiently and effectively to survive financially. They and their lenders, who also have significant stakes in the success of a project, must plan and develop every parcel to provide maximum utilization and minimum spoilage. Although they may go astray, they cannot reach the level of the political game where pressures, passions and whims are likely to be decisive.

Counterproductive Policies

Urban Sprawl

Consider what has happened in connection with urban sprawl, words that tend to produce shock and consternation to planners and environmentalists and one of the conditions a national land use bill would supposedly have curtailed. Yet, these very same groups in spite of their professed abhorrence of the condition, are currently most responsible for increasing it. They continually and successfully propose zoning regulations that are creating more urban sprawl than ever before.

Urban sprawl usually denotes a spreading or scattering of construction. It refers to a kind of leap-frogging pattern of growth where new construction is not erected consecutively to existing development. It is an inevitable consequence of urbanization, and will occur under any system of private or even public ownership, since vacant land next to a development may not be appropriate or desirable for use at a particular time.

Sprawling development is usually not advantageous to builders. They generally seek to build consecutively because most of their customers, both home buyers and renters, prefer being near existing development.[1] This is borne out by the fact that land abutting development almost invariably sells for more than land farther away. Also, to accommodate their purchasers, most of whom do not have or want to spend the extra money required to purchase larger lots, builders will tend in most instances to conserve on the size of vacant lots, and as a consequence, their normal practices will operate to save land and the distance between houses.

All of this is in sharp contrast to the impact of current zoning practices, which are probably creating more sprawl and wasting more precious land than ever before. Planners, in response to local opinion, are recommending land use regulations that are exceedingly harmful to the conservation of both land and energy.

First, many home owner and environmentally oriented groups

throughout the country, aided and abetted by planners, are causing the passage of much stricter density limitations requiring fewer homes per acre and curtailing development of garden apartments and high rises. They may demand, for example, a regulation allowing only two houses per acre instead of four or five, which necessarily causes greater housing spread and increases travel distance to and from home. Although these laws are intended to provide more open space, the bigger lots are still privately owned and the public has no more access to them than it does to the smaller lots.

Second, when the erection of garden apartments and high rises is restricted, people are forced to live in homes that occupy substantially more land per residential unit. A three-story apartment complex containing 250 to 300 units may occupy ten acres. It may require 80 to 100 acres to house the same number of families in homes. In effect, each floor of an apartment building adds to the supply of land.

Reducing density and limiting multifamily structures will waste hundreds of square miles within the country. If some of the dire predictions for our environmental future are even partially correct, we may someday need all of this land just to feed ourselves.

Third, there is considerable effort to limit the creation of new shopping facilities, which by being closer to residences lessen the use of the automobile.

Fourth, when communities restrict the erection of housing, developers are forced to build in places where they will encounter less resistance, usually the more rural and outlying sections. Thus, since the imposition of severer zoning regulations in the city of San Diego within the last several years, there has been considerably more building in the county, and the new construction is more distant than ever from shopping and employment.

Some of the other undesirable results of public land planning and zoning include the misuse of land, increased cost of housing, curtailment of competition, and breeding of corruption.

Misusing the Land

The modern world demands a high degree of expertise. Why then are we so willing to allow eminently unqualified people to have a voice in the development of the land? If the experts in this field are the builders and the developers, why, paradoxically, does zoning require them to submit their proposals for final decision to the public and its representatives?

Consider a situation that occurred in San Diego. One of the country's leading shopping center developers had sought since 1973 to build a major shopping and housing complex in a northern portion of the city. After substantial changes were made, the concept of the center was finally approved in May 1975 by the City Council. This approval, however, was subject to the requirement that the city's planning commission, comprised of private citizens appointed by the mayor and council, make the final decision on the actual design and placement of buildings and on other facets of the plan. The planning commission's deliberations are open to the public, and residents of the city were assured that they would have a strong role in the planning of the center.

The idea is preposterous. If people have reservations about placing their cares and concerns in the hands of general practitioners instead of specialists, they should be outraged at the prospect of entrusting it to those who have virtually no understanding at all. Some individuals do have specialized knowledge in architecture and design, but experience discloses that such persons stay away from zoning hearings, or if they do participate, it is to look after their own interests. Unfortunately, those with an axe to grind, local busybodies, and professional joiners have the most time for involvement. It is absurd to give an important role to those who have no stake in the success of a venture and may even prefer its demise. I have attended zoning hearings where home owners, whose combined knowledge of development would easily fit on the head of a pin, condemned complex plans prepared by highly skilled specialists. Worst of all, local authorities may weigh such comments heavily because they emanate from sources with a powerful weapon: the ability to vote them out of office.

Invariably, city planners and councilmen try to upgrade proposed developments. One gets the impression that residents want only Taj Mahals to be built in "their" municipalities. Developers seek to pass on the cost of upgrading by raising prices or rents. If market conditions do not allow for increases, the projects become economically unfeasible and are not erected. Production is thereby reduced, and this also causes prices or rents to rise.

Another possibility is that the developer will compensate for the added expense by reducing the quantity or quality of other

amenities. He may attempt to offset the cost of required park dedications, special architectural treatment, or lower density by, say,
lessening the amount of insulation and soundproofing or the quality
of the windows, doors, plumbing, heating, fixtures, etc.

The developer may still proceed in spite of the fact that his horse
has been turned into a camel and the market may not be as favorable
for camels. At least one reason for making such a decision is to save
the huge expenditures that probably were made in rezoning the
property. These expenses as well as those incurred in holding or
optioning the land might be lost if the project were abandoned.

The foregoing describes zoning in action and suggests the difference between the private and public planning process. The owners
of any business have to conduct it with maximum efficiency; otherwise their profits will diminish or disappear. They must purchase
and produce with minimal waste. Above all, they must create something consumers will buy at a price that includes a profit.

No such limitations confine the public regulators. They make
decisions for a large variety of reasons, and efficiency is rarely a
primary one, for there is little they can personally gain from
encouraging it. As a result, land use regulation causes the waste of
much land and resources.

High Rents

Consider the case of two Texas cities only 242 miles apart, Dallas
and Houston. Dallas has been zoned since the early thirties and
Houston has never had any zoning. Both have similar economic
statistics. There is one major exception, however; the cost of rent.
Apartment rentals in Houston are distinctly lower than Dallas,[2]
because in Houston the supply of land for apartments is not restricted by planning and political considerations. The absence of
zoning in Houston, by lowering rents, has benefited enormously the
environment of the average person. When, however, public regulation removes certain land from production, it decreases supply and
thereby raises the cost of shelter.

The Curtailment of Competition

In the absence of controls on production, there is usually a significant vacancy rate in the Houston rental market. However, construc-

tion still is more likely to continue there than elsewhere because builders do not have political as well as economic barriers to overcome. The experience of that city bears this out; apartment buildings continue to be produced in spite of the vacancy rates.

The basic reason is that the developer of each new project believes that he can provide something different or better than what is currently available and will be able, therefore, to attract people to rent his housing in preference to that of his competitors. He has detected some void in the market and believes he can satisfy it and still obtain a profitable return. This may involve providing extra amenities, larger rooms, more green space or recreational facilities, or perhaps lower rent. It requires skill, ingenuity, innovation, and much time and effort on the part of the developer. This is the means by which enormously valuable services are rendered the consuming public, without cost, by highly productive and skilled people. There is no government agency that can possibly provide or demand these benefits.

In housing or any other product, the consumer is dominant when competition abounds for it provides maximum choice. Governmental restrictions impair that process and reduce production, thereby weighing the scales in favor of sellers as against the interests of buyers.

An Invitation to Corruption

In 1972 the New York Times quoted William T. Cahill, then governor of New Jersey, as saying his state's zoning and land use laws "invited corruption" and were a "temptation" for extortions and kickbacks.[3] Surely the evidence from state after state has borne out his contention—with criminal charges implicating mayors, councilmen, county commissioners, and other local officials across the land. Corrupt politicians everywhere recognize zoning as a highly lucrative source of graft. It is dismaying to recognize that at times consumer demand can only be satisfied by paying off city hall.

The Failures of Zoning

Because they cannot comprehend market forces as businessmen do, planners, public officials, and politicians will tend to allow development where it is not feasible and prohibit it where it is. This will result in curtailment of much development, and will consequently be harmful to the vast numbers in this country dependent on new construction for their earnings, livelihood, and well-being. It will lead to unemployment and business slowdown, and tax revenues will decrease. Zoning already curtails entirely too much development; greater regulation will prevent even more.

Zoning has been a colossal flop because it is supposed to do things it cannot do. The same problems and failures will prevail under any system of government planning.

What, for instance, is the "right" mix of homes and apartments? How much industry is "too much?" Where is business to be allowed, and what kinds? Sections of Chicago are zoned so that a university is permitted, although a book store is not. You can open a shoe repair shop, grocery, drug store, or delicatessen, but not an art gallery, hardware or ice cream store. What Solomon's skill can split hairs like that?

The rationale is that planners envisioned quiet, serene shopping areas, limited to pedestrian traffic patronizing "mom and pop" stores. They could not possibly foresee that the regulations they wrote in the 1950s to keep out supermarkets would be helpless in the 1960s to exclude the newly conceived neighborhood minisupermarkets, depending almost entirely on automobile traffic from after dawn to midnight. They qualified as small grocery stores.

Zoning is replete with comparable failures. Chicago's zoning ordinance at the time of its adoption received rave reviews and is still considered technically one of the best. It still causes absurd, unjust, and undesirable results. Similar consequences can be expected from other public regulation of land use.

Notes

1. See Siegan, *Controlling Other People's Property Through Covenants, Zoning, State and Federal Regulation*, 5 ENVIRONMENTAL LAW 385, 459-461 (1975).

2. SIEGAN, LAND USE WITHOUT ZONING 117-121 (Lexington, Mass: Lexington Books 1972).

3. *Cahill Weighs Legislation To Ban Corruption*, N.Y. Times, Sept. 22, 1972, at 1.

2 Regulation: How Much Is Too Much?

Controlling Other People's Property

Everyone wants to live under optimum conditions, and one means to that end is to control the use of other people's property. The United States presently faces the question of how far that control should extend; should it be confined to one's own home, or to the neighborhood, city, state, or entire country?

Probably from time immemorial, man has sought to select his neighbors and that has influenced his choice of housing. Price differentials in housing create neighborhoods in this country catering to different income levels. Similarly, the rich or powerful in the socialist countries do not live in the same buildings or areas as their less fortunate comrades.

Builders have long satisfied consumer desires by imposing restrictive covenants (or deed restrictions) on lots within their subdivision. *Restrictive covenants* are private legal agreements that usually prohibit for specified periods the use of lots for anything other than the erection of houses. They would prevent apartments and commercial and industrial uses within a residential subdivision. Restrictive covenants are in principle legally valid and binding. They are upheld by the courts except when they impose highly onerous restraints, such as racial restrictions, which are totally unenforcible. Control under the covenants extends only within the boundaries of the subdivision and not outside of it. Individual subdivisions are limited in size, constituting generally a fraction of the area of a city or town. For that reason, subdivision controls were inadequate to those who insisted upon regulation of other property within a municipality—seemingly to safeguard their own.

And so, along came zoning, and since it is a political process, it enabled people living at one end of a city or town to influence or even determine the use of property at the other end. In spite of the increasing severity of its controls—its early proponents would hardly recognize them—local zoning has also turned out to be insufficient.

11

"Don't Californicate Oregon! Don't Californicate Colorado!" These are among the battle cries of environmentalists seeking to control land use within an entire state, most of which they will never personally live in, visit, see, or even hear or read about. They seek to forbid the use of land for purposes they do not approve of—and most development fits that description. California's unforgiveable sin is providing too well for the housing needs of human beings. "Visit, but don't stay" describes the mood. Its proponents might next advocate entry permits or visas to travel within *their* states.

If they are not successful, the next step in the process will be at the federal level, and if national land use legislation is adopted, that is where people aggrieved by state regulation will seek relief. Washington is where both those who want more and those who prefer fewer controls will turn, and one of these groups must necessarily lose. Theoretically, 49 percent of the American people may be strongly opposed to certain laws regulating land use, but until they achieve majority status, they will be able to do little more than grin and bear it.

As environmentalists are beginning to learn, an energy crisis, a recession, serious unemployment, or general swings of the pendulum may convert in their view a state legislature or the Congress from benevolency to tyranny, from wisdom to stupidity. Relying upon the state may be akin to playing Russian roulette.

The proposition that government should regulate the use of land inevitably leads to Washington. Yet, this long and tortuous course is unnecessary; the homestead can be preserved and protected with little government involvement. That tried and proven private device, restrictive covenants, will do the job.

In the absence of zoning, developers generally will impose the covenants on subdivisions in accordance with the desires of their customers. Home owners will thereby control the use of someone else's property—but only within their own immediate neighborhood. More precisely, the controls under the covenants are mutual ones, creating equal burdens and benefits for all those within a subdivision covered by them. Everyone has the same right to enforce and the same obligation to comply with the restrictions. Unlike zoning, one's influence over another's property is not dependant on one's influence over politicians.

The actual experience of Houston and other areas without zoning shows that communities can function well, and the values of homes and other real estate can be maintained and enhanced without giving home owners much more protection than they are accorded by restrictive covenants.

Regulation: A Double Standard

Why is government regulation so reprehensible when it limits speech or press and so desirable when it controls property? Why is government so tyrannical and stupid in the one case and so benevolent and wise in the other?

Apparently, many believe that a leopard can change its spots, depending on its intended victim. Our society treats political rights and property rights in an enormously different way. There is little control of one and much of the other. Government needs relatively little excuse to restrict the use of property as the experience of zoning demonstrates. But when it comes to civil rights set forth in the Constitution, as the late Justice Hugo Black once wrote about free speech, "only the gravest abuses endangering paramount interests give occasion for permissible limitation".[1]

Few have better understanding of government abuses than the many organizations in the country dedicated to protecting civil and political rights. However, they never seem to apply this knowledge and prefer to look the other way when governmental agencies effectively deprive people of property, the fruit of their labor, savings, energy, and knowledge. They strenuously fight against the imposition of a minimal fine when political liberties are involved, and stand absolutely mute when the most arbitrary zoning and environmental restrictions reduce by hundreds or thousands of dollars the values of property owned by people of average means.

Yet, as Economists Professor Ronald Coase of the University of Chicago Law School observed in a paper that has attracted some national attention: "For most people in most countries (and perhaps in all countries) the provision of food, clothing and shelter is a good deal more important than the provision of the 'right ideas,' even assuming we know which they are."[2] Professor Coase was discussing the sharp distinction made in the treatment between the ordinary market for goods and services and what he referred to as the "market for ideas" in which he included the exercise of religious beliefs, speech, and writing. The government's motivation, judgment, competency, or efficiency are good or bad, it appears, contingent on which market is involved.

Clearly there is a double standard operating. Possibly the grossest example of it is provided by the editorial writers of our most prominent liberal newspapers. When press freedom is the topic, they have no peer in pointing out the sins and absurdities of government. That critical talent is strangely muted when proposed new economic and social programs are discussed. We learn in these editorials about the wisdom of government. These papers may simply be defending their own self-interest in the acquisition and sale of news, which on analysis would seem to have more to do with the rights of property than with press. Why then are they so oblivious to the rights of others who similarly seek to acquire and sell or develop their products?

Newspapers are not alone in this selective approach. In recent decades, the U.S. Supreme Court has been elevating political and civil rights and downgrading economic and property rights. For a long period in our history, the court was prone to declare unconstitutional laws interfering with the opportunity to engage in business or own property. In the late 1930s, the Supreme Court changed direction and since then has been most reluctant to invalidate economic regulatory legislation. It displays no hesitancy when speech or press is involved. The country, as a consequence, now follows a course of unequal constitutional rights. Although nowhere in the Constitution does it say that certain rights shall be mightier than others, that is in effect, how that document is being interpreted. Despite their seeming antipathy to it, judges and editors favor *laissez-faire* in those areas they most use and best comprehend: writing and speaking. The priorities might be considerably different were other occupations or professions as influential in making the rules.

Maximum competition in the economic marketplace will allow for maximum satisfaction of consumer needs and desires, and provide consumers with new and better products at lower cost. By regulating these markets, we are giving the power of government to certain individuals to determine what will be produced or created and for whom, and that power must necessarily be used disadvantageously to some, possibly most—as would occur if certain ideas were censored.

Thus, it is becoming readily apparent that by restricting the use of land through zoning, government harms the consumers of housing as much as the owners of land. For a family struggling to maintain financial solvency, the cost of such government regulation in increased rents can be a severe hardship.

Less Control—Less Corruption

An example of legislation that has enormous potential for moral or legal corruption was proposed national land use legislation. Under it, hundreds of federal and state legislators, their staffs, and virtually countless government office holders would have been added to the already enormous number of people presently involved in land use regulation. They would have been expected to make decisions affecting the lives and fortunes of a great many, including, of course, their own. And this is where the problem would have arisen. One need not be much of a sage to predict that many, if not most, of these decisions would have been made to benefit the personal interests of the decision maker.

The experience of local land use regulation or zoning tells us what would happen. In the zoning process, politicians, planners, and bureaucrats have been able to feather their nests by favoring those with the greatest political power, the loudest political voices, and/or the readiest cash. Political contributions and graft are not the sole means of wrongdoing, although graft has been one of the factors greatly influencing the outcome of zoning controversies; there are a great many other factors and pressures that also affect results.

Consider, for example, the case of the politician who seeks higher office or wishes to maintain his present office. The support of particular organizations and individuals may be much more rewarding than obtaining a developer's money or political contributions. By loudly condemning and voting against requests of builders and developers, these politicians tend to attract the support of some organizations that can muster volunteers to canvass precincts, do clerical work, mail letters, and help create a favorable image.

The purpose of obtaining campaign contributions and sometimes graft is to pay for exactly these services, and many politicians have learned that it is just as easy to obtain them through certain approaches to the regulation of land use. What is wrong with this? The same objection as in taking graft; the politician is furthering his own self-interest rather than judging on the merits of the particular case.

Nevertheless, none of the laws affecting campaign contributions can control this form of moral corruption.

Less regulation results in less corruption. In Houston, which has no zoning, the local councilman cannot impose or remove restrictions on any land for the benefit of those politically or economically strong and influential. Unlike their counterparts elsewhere, the politicians there have minimal power to produce windfall profits for some developers and home owners, and wipeouts for others.

What is perhaps the most unfortunate aspect of regulatory legislation is that graft frequently leads to better results for society than the less tainted variety of politics. Graft may be the only means of removing restrictions and allowing market forces to operate, a shocking and rather shameful situation. Thus, in view of today's housing problems, one may well ask, whose actions are more socially undesirable, the untouchable legislator who votes to reject the construction of housing or the graft taker who approves it.

It is indeed distressing to speculate on how many major developments came about only as a result of the payment of graft or fees to certain parties. Can society justify creation or maintenance of a regulatory system where consumer demand can quite often only be saitsfied by resorting to illegal or morally and socially reprehensible practices?

Helping the Few and Harming the Many

In Houston 10,000 Ralph Naders could not have accomplished as much for the tenants of that city as have the builders. Rents remain relatively low and apartments are plentiful and varied. Yet, a major reason builders have done so well for the people is not because they are watched and hounded, but for exactly opposite reasons. Houston has no zoning and as a result there are far fewer legal restraints on producers of housing than in the other major municipalities, all of which do have zoning.

That city employs as its principal restraint the most effective of them all: competition. This means builders compete with each other and try to outdo one another in an effort to gain the favor of the housing consumer. What occurs there in the case of shelter is no different from that which takes place whenever and wherever competition reigns. Who can possibly serve the housewife as efficiently, effectively, and as well as the local supermarket? The average supermarket is a shrine of consumerism, displaying its wares and goodwill so that the consumer will buy there and not elsewhere. It pays a serious penalty for mistreating the customer: loss of patronage.

But some people have difficulties with sellers, and thus there are complaints about housing in Houston. A typical reaction is to call for government regulation to correct the difficulties. Experience shows that this is clearly the wrong response. Regulation either will not solve the problem, or if it does, it may well create other and more serious ones.

These are two examples illustrating this conclusion reported in recent news stories:

1. There is no regulation more humanely intended than usury laws. They are designed to protect against unsavory practices of lenders and to prevent the elevation of interest rates. In some states in 1973 and 74, they were instead preventing persons from purchasing new and used homes. The states in question were those that had usury ceilings below prevailing interest rates. Thus Illinois had an 8 percent rate when lenders could obtain a better return on other more secure investments, or on mortgages in states with higher ceilings. The Illinois legislators in time raised the ceiling but not before many had been seriously disadvantaged.

Nor was there ever any need for the usury law in the first place. Try as they might to obtain higher rates, it is doubtful that any one of the many existing savings and loan institutions or banks could have raised rates above the competitive level. The few possible exceptions hardly warrant a law that at times virtually can cut off the supply of financing.

2. There will be higher prices and worse conditions in mobile home parts in some parts of the country because of proposed regulations that elevate the standards for land area, density, and other requirements for new parks. These standards increase substantially the cost of developing a mobile home park. Consequently, fewer parks will be constructed, and there will be less supply and competition than would occur in the absence of such regulations.

The same principle holds true for most other governmental regulations; on the whole they harm much more than help. They make it more difficult for people of average and less income to buy many products, thereby operating as effectively as the usury law did in Illinois to prevent people from satisfying their needs and desires.

Creating and Destroying Property Values

Federal and state governments build and pay for expressways and roads. These installations make it possible for the land adjoining and nearby to be developed and to rise substantially in value. Some argue that these governments therefore should control the use of this property. Others also contend that the increase in value should belong to the taxpayers, since it is the "creation of the community." Certain groups go even further, insisting that the increase in value of land, arising as it does from the effects of an entire community, should belong to the community and not to the individuals who might hold title.

These arguments have been making the rounds nationally and internationally for a long time. They are now being advanced to justify much greater federal and state intervention in the use and development of the land. However, the position they espouse contains a number of weaknesses:

1. By the same logic, the federal and state governments would also be able to regulate and take away the profits from businesses in the cities and towns that arise when roads are installed. Carried to its ultimate conclusion, a "but-for" argument can be made to socialize virtually all activities in the country since they could not be conducted except for the protection afforded by the military and police.

Proponents should consider the reverse side of their position. When the government's programs destroy or remove wealth, is this cause for eliminating its authority? If that were the rule, anarchy might at times reign. And the government might go broke making restitution.

People's prosperity can be attributed to a wide scope of public and private activities that constitute the "community." Our market economy makes possible the roads, highways, military, and police, and it would be strange indeed if their existence were a pretext to eliminate or curtail the system that created them.

The arguments complicate and confuse a simple situation. The government owns and controls that which it pays for: the roads and the highways. The road program, like others, is a function of government operating to augment growth and well being.

2. Economic conditions are more responsible for appreciation of value than is road building. A twenty lane new highway in the Alaskan tundra would have little effect while the installation of a

street in a populous city will have a great impact on property values. The difference is attributable to market forces.

3. Governments install roads because there is no private agency able to fund the process and acquire the needed land. The same reason does not apply to the use and development of the adjoining land that can be carried out privately. Any reasonable allocation of labor would separate the two functions. If there is another way to achieve the optimum use and development of property, it would be ridiculous to force government regulation just because its actions made construction possible.

4. The argument presumes that land and property benefit when roads are constructed. But what about those that lose value when this occurs? For example, property values in the downtown areas of the country have diminished over the years due to the development of outlying shopping centers made possible by the building of new highways. The movement to the suburbs, also induced by these new arteries, reduced many property values in the major cities as people moved away. When roads are extended, existing enterprises lose business to the new ones opening in the developing areas. They could well claim the government's efforts harmed them.

If government is to control the areas that its actions cause to appreciate in value, it should not control places where it has created the opposite effect. And if it is to be compensated by those for whom it has created benefits, it should be obligated to reimburse those for whom it has diminished values. This general principle, if applied in practice, would create a mind-bobbling accounting system with never ending controversies over values and cause and effect.

Other government programs would get involved. The FHA is also responsible for growth of suburbia and many property owners in the big cities likewise would have a claim against it. Suburban growth can even be attributed to the Federal Reserve's easy money policies, which made mortgage money plentiful.

5. Nor is it fair for controls to be imposed on an after-the-fact basis. Federal or state control of adjoining property was never made a condition for the installation of the roads. Had this issue been submitted to the legislature at the time these programs were adopted, they might have been defeated. To accomplish this objective subsequently is highly prejudicial to those who purchased or began developing property in reliance on the provisions of the original legislation.

The No-Growth Movement

Remember the no-growth movement? It was in full swing in 1973 when its proponents were loudly proclaiming the blessings that would result if the nation's economic growth were halted. Through no fault of theirs, and far beyond their greatest expectations, they have succeeded, However, very few others are cheering.

The country's economic growth has terminated, and the unpleasant consequences are readily apparent. We face unemployment, business slowdown, and failures. The economic outlook is not favorable. People will be spending much more time at leisure and in the parks, but unfortunately not by choice.

The prime target of the no-growthers seemed to be the building industry. Land use regulations were adopted in many areas, severely curtailing development of residential, commercial, and industrial structures. Developers were condemned as scoundrels, denying land to trees, lagoons, animals, and of course, nature lovers. And the latter, insisted some, included just about everyone.

Today, however, a complete change in direction is called for; economic growth should be strongly encouraged. A most effective means to that end is to rescind the multitude of laws that control development of the land. This would include local and state zoning, and the proposed federal land use controls. All operate to limit freedom to use and develop property. Freedom in the marketplace is a standing invitation for man to exercise his creative, productive, and developmental instincts, and that translates into more business activity and employment. There is no force on earth that will encourage production and distribution more than that much maligned profit motive.

How about compromising on some sort of "controlled growth"? A true compromise is rarely possible because government usually has the final power to decide on the terms. That would mean that voters, politicians, planners, do-gooders, and do-badders would be making decisions that can be made much better by those who have the incentive, knowledge, ingenuity, and energy to create and produce. Regrettably politicians all too often profit when they prevent or curtail the production of goods and services.

Does it make a difference that some areas continue to retain their antigrowth policies? There is little question that it does. I am not aware of any communities in this country that are economic islands.

If there are no local developers and workers to do the work, it will be done by those who reside in other communities, and all business activity has a multiplier effect that spreads and has impact many miles beyond its source. Accordingly, restrictions anywhere can contribute to economic difficulties.

Even the most seemingly innocuous regulations can hinder development. A yard, area, or height limitation might make economically unfeasible the erection of a certain structure. If a tract of land on a major thoroughfare is zoned for, say, a two-story residential building, it will remain vacant unless a developer is willing to invest in that kind of structure. The more restrictions on the use of property, the fewer are the opportunities to develop it, and, consequently, the best way to cause property to be utilized is to eliminate these restrictions. In Houston the absence of zoning has allowed for much development that never would have occurred in its presence.

It is almost frightening therefore to contemplate the result to the economy of previously proposed state or national land use regulation laws under which enormous areas would be restricted in accordance with the dictates, plans, and guesses of politicians and planners. They could not possibly have the insights and knowledge of those in the development business, and, as a result, would invariably make many decisions that would prevent building.

The antigrowth movement is incompatible with individual freedom for it requires maximum government coercion to succeed. It is equally detrimental to the people's pocketbooks. There can be no better reasons for letting it remain an historical oddity.

No-Growth: An Additional Cost

We reject all growth that is not profitable. We reject new development that does not pay its way in taxes. There are not edicts from General Motors or United States Steel, nor the Bank of America. These declarations paraphrase the words and actions of many municipalities and citizens throughout the country who are seeking to stop further growth on the grounds, among others, that new development raises taxes for existing residents. Interestingly enough, they come from sources that are continuously criticizing and condemning builders and developers for being profit motivated.

There are battles raging today on many fronts concerning the cost of additional growth. Some municipalities, as well as some environmentalist and conservationist groups, have produced studies showing that growth does not pay its way and the pro-development forces have countered with equally respectable studies showing precisely the opposite. Statistically, it appears to be a stalemate, although neither side appears ready to acknowledge the validity of the other's studies.

Not too long ago it was rare to find environmentalists and conservationists arguing the growth issue on such pragmatic grounds. Their position then was seemingly confined to the virtues per se of pure air and water, open space and the natural terrain. In contending that nature and the wild are also good for the pocketbook, they have emerged into the world of pragmatism and their position is highly vulnerable on this basis.

The studies relating to the cost of growth are generally cost-revenue analyses, in which the cost of servicing new development and its occupants is compared to the revenue derived therefrom. There are many difficulties in compiling all of the factors involved. What such studies overlook are the benefits that result generally to business, the employment, and the tax revenues from construction and use of housing and related facilities, and these are extensive. Not only do the builders and their workers benefit financially, but so also do businessmen and their employees, members of the professions, and wage earners in general.

The multiplier effect of business transactions will create advantages for many people not involved in construction. The rise in personal income should at least overall offset increased costs caused by growth. More earnings means more tax revenues to the advantage of all taxpayers. Obviously there will be greater benefits in some towns than in others. On a regional basis, however, the overall financial impact of growth should be clearly favorable.

Furthermore, the growth issue raises the fundamental question of whether it is desirable or permissible in an open society for barriers and walls to be erected preventing the mobility of people. Whatever benefits those who got there first derive from their restrictive policies will be at the expense directly of those who are excluded by them. Restrictions upon growth make existing housing more expensive by curtailing supply of housing accommodations to the disadvantage of those who want to buy or rent. Some people will have to remain in less desirable environmental conditions so that others may enjoy more desirable ones.

Justice Roberts of the Pennsylvania Supreme Court summed up the competition for space in a 1970 opinion that invalidated two- and three-acre zoning in that state: "The question posed is whether the township can stand in the way of natural forces which send our growing population into hitherto undeveloped areas in search of a comfortable place to live."[3]

For those persons and groups truly concerned about the impact of growth on real estate taxes, there is a better way of augmenting collections: remove all land use restrictions. By removing such restrictions, cities and towns will be encouraging the location of developments that are highly profitable for the tax base, such as factories, shopping centers and high rises, all of which yield substantial tax revenues and cost relatively little to service. The plants and centers produce none and the high rises relatively few children, and schools are by far the most expensive of municipal services, typically accounting for two-thirds to three-fourths of real estate tax bills.

By limiting growth, towns and cities also limit the number of potential shoppers, consequently deterring the construction of shopping centers. Housing limitations may likewise exclude workers for industry, and thereby prevent location of that source for revenues.

Problems of the Poor

A strange phenomenon of our times is the attitude of local office holders who identify themselves with the cause of the poor, and at the same time insist on curbing growth. In San Diego, for example, many politicians whose hearts continually bleed for the downtrodden are among the strongest supporters of a restricted growth policy, which can only be harmful to the poor.

The two positions are totally incompatible, and one begins to wonder how genuine their commitment is, and to whom or what it is. The answer may lie in the working of both sides of the political street, plying the rich and young with "no-growth" promises and the poor with lots of rhetoric. Plainly these politicians are not heeding the advice of the bumper stickers that urged us to "eschew obfuscation."

Friends of the poor should be working hard to overcome governmental restrictions that curtail production, and some are. One public body that adopted a clear position on the issue is the San Diego County Board of Public Welfare. On May 2, 1975, in a written recommendation to the county's Board of Supervisors, it said the slow growth policies of the city and county were "at cross purposes with the goals and objectives of the Board of Public Welfare."

Its statement continued: "The elimination of poor or substandard housing accommodations demands an immediate change in the county's growth policy. This policy is acting to restrict the supply of housing available to poor people."

Regarding the means for achieving satisfactory housing for the poor, the statement discussed both subsidized and privately financed housing and concluded that the former has not been particularly successful: "It is very expensive and has served only a small proportion of those in need."

The board referred to a report made by the Federal Department of Housing and Urban Development that the average subsidized apartment unit cost 20 percent more to construct than a comparable unit privately financed. This meant, the Welfare Board reasoned, that about 20 percent fewer dwellings could be built by the government than if the same amount of money had been invested in the private market.

It concluded that: "The greatest hope for improving the living conditions of the ill-housed poor in our community, and at the same time substantially relieving the financial burden placed on the Board of Supervisor's budget (and the taxpayers of San Diego) appears to be through the private market; specifically through the filtering process."

Filtering is the chain of moves to new or different living quarters triggered by the construction and occupancy of a new unit. The leading source available on this process is the study conducted by the Survey Research Center at the University of Michigan, published as a monograph, "New Homes and Poor People."[4]

This study, conducted in seventeen metropolitan areas in the mid-1960s, determined that for every 1,000 new housing units built, there are over 3,500 relocations, of which an average of 330 are by families defined as poor and 950 by moderate income families, the next lowest economic category. The moves will be made presumably to better housing on the assumption that "if they move, they benefit." The Welfare Board considers the filtering process "the only proven viable provider of low cost housing for low and moderate income families."

According to the board, the number of building permits issued in San Diego County in 1974 was 24,000 fewer than in 1972. Of the reasons cited for the decrease, one was the restricted growth policy. Using the statistics provided in the Michigan study, the board figured that had this amount of new construction occurred, better housing would have been available for over 31,000 poor- and moderate-income families. By contrast, it pointed out, local government was pursuing the idea of building only 600 homes for the needy.

The statement added that a great deal of pressure for subsidized housing arose from the notion that "for some reason, poor people should live in brand new houses. The emphasis instead, should be on enabling poor people to exercise upward mobility by removing the barriers to improved housing."

The board described these barriers as forms of land use and building regulation, specifically impediments to new construction set up by the California Coastal Commission, Environmental Quality Act, zoning regulations, construction processing delays, and the substantial fees demanded of builders to obtain permits.

The board's analysis illustrates powerfully how harmful land use regulation is to the well-being of lower income people.

Rent Controls

It is a good bet that growth controls will lead to rent controls. If there is a strong demand for apartments and construction is not allowed to respond, rents can skyrocket. There will then be strong pressure for a law to reduce or stabilize them. That is not a scenario invented to fight antigrowth laws. Some proponents of development curbs fully acknowledge this, regarding rent regulation as part of the package.

Petitions were circulated in 1974 in the cities of San Diego County, California and the county itself to place growth control initiatives on the various ballots. The proposed initiatives contained a provision specifically recognizing that legislation for rent controls would be necessary to complement the growth ordinances. (None of the petitions succeeded either for lack of signatures or technical inadequacies.)

Rent control itself will further reduce building and thereby intensify the problems it is intended to alleviate. Prospective developers will be deterred from investing in new construction when subject to profit limitations. Even if controls are inapplicable to new construction, builders are still likely to decide against undertaking these ventures because of possible extension in the future.

Rent ceilings also will cause landlords to diminish the supply of apartments by converting to condominiums, or abandoning them as they become unprofitable.

Much of the effect on rents will be strictly illusory. As rents are fixed, landlords will seek to compensate for cost increases by reducing services, repairs, maintenance, and replacement, causing buildings to deteriorate more rapidly. While the price remains the same, it will be purchasing a lesser quality of housing.

This might not happen to families with lawyers on call, but it is increasingly probable as income levels descend and landlord battling becomes progressively harder. Those struggling daily for economic survival can hardly afford to take the risk, real or imagined, of having services cut off or being locked out, even if both are illegal. Rent controls, consequently, provide little help for poorer tenants who, one would think, should be their prime beneficiaries.

By curtailing supply, the growth and rent laws would make tenants dependant on either the strict enforcement of rent laws or the conscience of the landlord. Families would be deprived of their strongest weapon against landlord abuse, the opportunity to move, since there would be little or nothing else available.

But could those of average or less income, even in the absence of such laws, afford new homes or apartments? The answer is that new construction provides housing opportunities for more than just those who occupy it. In moving to a new unit, the buyer or renter vacates a unit for occupancy by others, who in turn do likewise, and this continues on down the line, creating a chain of moves. About 50 percent of the moves that occur annually in this country to different residences are attributable to this process. The University of Michigan's Survey Research Center study has shown that for every move into new construction, there are, as a result, two and one-half moves into older units.

The unfortunate experiences of cities with rent control apparently has been heard even by would-be believers. Although students enthusiastically led Berkeley and Cambridge to vote them in, the ranks may by now have changed their minds. Another city with considerable student population (from Stanford University), Palo Alto, California, decided the issue differently. Rent control was soundly defeated there by a vote of 14,480 to 5,711 or 72 percent to 28 percent. Seven of the nine-person, liberal-oriented City Council opposed it. Four joined in a statement that "the self-policing, self-regulation of a free market under general law serves all interests best."

The result might, of course, be entirely different after a prolonged period of growth regulation, especially as the demand for apartments keeps multiplying.

Laws could be passed to (1) provide huge government housing subsidies, (2) jail landlords who do not scrupulously observe rent ceilings, (3) curb conversion of apartments to condominiums, and (4) penalize landlords who abandon buildings. But when these fail or create new problems, then what?

Housing Ordinances

Building Codes

It is hard to conceive of a better candidate for regulation than the safety of buildings. Human life is involved and every precaution is warranted to prevent builders from creating, willingly or unwillingly, conditions that will endanger it. That, we are told, is the reason why building codes are adopted. A building code is supposed to be a series of standards and specifications intended to protect occupants of buildings against fire, structural collapse, and other hazards.

These codes are usually passed and enforced by local governments, subject to the final authority of the state. There are four national organizations of building officials that prepare and publish recommended model building codes. These groups employ experts to research and test materials and methods. Almost all municipalities use the recommended codes as a basis for their own building codes but frequently modify them to suit local conditions. Some of the larger cities draft their own codes.

It sounds simple, clear, and proper. The difficulty is that building codes are among the most abused regulations in the country. After an exhaustive study, a Presidential (Douglas) Commission, in a report published in 1968, concluded that "alarms sounded over the past years about the building code situation have been justified. If anything, the case has been understated. The situation calls for a drastic overhaul, both technically and intergovernmentally."[5]

The codes have required construction and installations far beyond the needs of safety. The municipalities start with the model codes and frequently add substantial numbers of extras. Building is consequently much more expensive than it should be. Some construction has been stopped unneccessarily, and people of lesser means have fewer housing opportunities. The principal causes for code abuses are:

1. Many localities use the codes not only for safety standards, but to determine the kind of structures they want erected, usually more costly ones. In this respect, the codes are used to exclude inexpensive housing and thereby less wealthy home owners and tenants who would occupy them.

2. Both the politicians who adopt them and the officials who enforce them frequently have exercised uninformed and arbitrary judgments as to what will or will not provide adequate protection.

3. Some unions and contractors have successfully lobbied to require excessive standards that will create more work and require more materials. They have fought the introduction of technology that would lessen the use of labor and materials.

Although studies have been conducted, there has been no overall analysis of the economic consequences of the codes. To determine their worth and effectiveness fully would require a comparison with construction in areas where they do not exist. What happens when there are no building codes? Do buildings collapse or burn up?

Relatively few areas have no building codes. One such is the unincorporated section of Harris County, Texas. (Houston is located in this county, but does have a typical building code.) Possibly 300,000 people live in the area of that county where building codes have never existed. (The county does have flood control regulations that sometimes affect construction.) The only properties subject to building regulation are those insured by FHA or VA, both of which do maintain construction requirements.

The rest of the county is not without any protection, however.

Private sources provide safeguards: First, it is in the interest of certain companies for buildings to be safe. Savings and loan associations and other lenders pass on the specifications of the buildings on which they lend money. They do not want their mortgage investment of twenty-five or more years to be jeopardized. Fire insurance companies refuse to cover fire traps, and the electrical utility will not extend service in a dangerous situation. Second, many portions of buildings come preassembled and because they are mass produced, have to accommodate the bulk of builders and lenders who will seek safe products. In addition, manufacturers can be legally liable for hazards they create. Last, builders are no more careless about human life than any other group. The vast number of people act with due consideration for the safety and well being of others. Furthermore, those in business who develop a bad reputation either among workers or customers are not likely to stay around very long.

Building codes demonstrate once again that government never seems able to find the line separating arbitrary from necessary regulation.

Minimum Housing Laws

Whenever middle-class "do-gooders" visit poor neighborhoods, they return insisting that something be done immediately. Understandably upset by what they have seen, they want the government to force the landlord to make numerous repairs and installations to upgrade living conditions. They usually demand the imposition of regulations that will compel owners to act more "humanely" toward tenants.

There is a tendency to blame the owner entirely for the bad conditions and totally ignore the responsibility of the tenants. It should be apparent, however, from public housing experience, where the landlord supposedly has nothing to gain from skimping, that tenants are not free of complicity. Unpleasant and even dangerous conditions exist in public housing that are entirely attributable to tenants. Those with such bad habits obviously also rent private accommodations. In such circumstances, new installations will benefit principally the installers.

Perhaps some limited health standards are justified, applying to both landlord and tenant. It is to be hoped that if enforced by the health department, little harm and possibly some good may result. Regulation greater than that, however, will create more problems for people who have enough already. This is why:

1. If the owner installs new equipment or rehabilitates the units, rents will have to rise to compensate for his cost or because the apartments would then command greater market value. Tenants will have to pay the increase although many already probably have rejected this choice by not moving into other quarters that have these amenities.

People with lower incomes must carefully budget it. If their rent is higher, there will be less for food, clothing, gasoline, fuel, etc. Perhaps they prefer Cadillacs to better living quarters—and who is to quarrel with that decision? People should have the option to live their own lives as they deem best.

Obviously housing in good repair looks better than that in bad condition. Raising housing standards, however, is another of those civic improvements financed almost entirely by those least able to: the lowest income groups.

2. Minimum housing laws have proven very difficult to enforce. In some instances, it would require an army to make the continual inspections that are necessary. In Laredo, Texas, for example, enforcement would lead to the demolition of a large portion of its housing, and that community has been reluctant to take such action. A similar attitude may exist in numerous localities throughout the country.

Adding to the problem is that the tenants may injure, destroy, or remove equipment, and it is often unfair to penalize the landlord for lack of compliance. A law that cannot be enforced justly is a bad one.

3. Housing ordinances, as is true of most regulations, start small but grow increasingly restrictive. As costs rise, low-income tenants have to divert more and more of their wages for rents, adding to their troubles. The difficulty is that minimum standards will never satisfy the civic groups whose well heeled members are more influenced by their own priorities and tastes than those of their alleged beneficiaries. And slum conditions are always ripe for an exposé by the news media.

In the initial days of urban renewal, its supporters proclaimed that the process would eliminate the slums. Many were demolished, but that did not solve the troubles of those who had lived in them. Most of those displaced either could not afford or did not want to pay for better accommodations. Many sought similarly priced housing and simply moved from one slum to another. Others went to fancier areas where they might then or in time double up, causing greater wear and tear on those buildings.

Rather than force rents upward through minimum housing regulations, efforts should go full speed ahead to lower them by removing legal barriers to increased production. Among other things, owners of rental properties should not be restricted in preserving their investment. They should, for example, be able to evict rent delinquent tenants or their cash flow will be imperiled. Courts in some states have prevented or delayed evictions of nonpaying tenants who complain they have not been provided with adequate repairs or services. Before such disputes are finally adjudicated, the owner may lose much income and incur many legal expenses although there is little or no fault on his part. Judges should exercise great caution in attempting to aid tenants in this manner.

Such rules place great financial pressure on landlords who must satisfy regular mortgage, tax, and maintenance obligations. As a result, fewer will invest in real estate and those who do will be more likely to abandon buildings or convert them to condominiums. A reduced supply will lead to worse, not better, conditions. It will harm tenants the most.

Density Requirements

How many people should live on an acre of land? It all depends on who answers—and, frequently, who asks.

There is much literature on the subject of *density*, that is, the number of dwelling units that should be erected within a specified area. No more unity exists among the authors than in the many cities and towns that confront the issue regularly when adopting and changing zoning regulations. Denisty requirements vary greatly between communities.

At public hearings in the Chicago suburbs, seemingly rational people have insisted that a density exceeding twenty apartments per acre would surely lead to slums. At other times, equally concerned residents virtually took oaths that five houses to the acre was the brink. Zoning is often decided on the basis of such fears. Yet, only twenty-five minutes away on Chicago's Gold Coast stood prestigious high rise apartments in areas zoned 400 units per acre. The incidence of crime was among the lowest and conditions among the best in the city. There are innumerable instances throughout the nation of highly successful high rise buildings catering to families of various income levels.

A principal exception is government sponsored public housing, and it is not limited to just tall buildings. Many families that occupy such housing are problem prone, with considerable delinquency. The difficulties arise from the residents, not the housing. Although they may be in the minority, such families can create serious problems for others as well as for the structure. Worst of all, the bad families keep out—or taint—the good.

High density among lower income groups does not preclude good housing. Jane Jacobs, in her book *The Death and Life of Great American Cities*, describes the North End, a modest-income section of Boston. It contained 275 units to the acre in 1959, yet was among the lowest in delinquency, disease, and infant mortality rates of that city. The only criticism leveled by a city planner to whom Mrs. Jacobs spoke was that there were too many people—and that apparently meant it was a slum. "You should have more slums like this," was Mrs. Jacobs' response.[6]

Congresswoman Leonor Sullivan of Missouri was surprised to discover extremely pleasant circumstances in high rises of Hong Kong that are jampacked with poor families. "There is order and control," she said in a speech several years ago. "The places are spotless, the people who live in them are buoyed in spirit and absolutely delighted with the step up the housing ladder to their very own private homes—even a single room for a family." What about those who did not behave? "They were kicked out."[7]

In America this kind of response occurs in new private rental developments, but is near impossible in public housing. The incentives are vastly different. In the latter, what Mrs. Sullivan suggests is an excessive compassion causes the retention of the problem family. The reaction of public housing managers, she points out, is, "How can we put them out? Where would they go?"

The fear of great density permeated nonzoned Houston's planning department in the late 1960s, when some high-density, single-family rental projects were erected. Houston has no density controls on rental units and the planners were concerned by projects having sixteen or more detached units to the acre, unusually concentrated by prevailing standards. The department recommended unsuccessfully to the City Council that density restrictions be imposed with respect to them.

The developments in question were being erected in black, ghetto type areas by private nonsubsidized investment, a rarity in this country. Such sections are usually devoid of new privately built housing. An important inducement for the developers was the opportunity afforded by large density to reduce land and construction costs. These projects have to date afforded good, inexpensive housing, and are usually fully occupied in spite of Houston's normally high vacancy rates.

Had the proposed restrictions been adopted, the increased costs probably would have prevented such projects from being built. The biggest losers would have been the many people denied this housing and forced to continue living in their less desirable quarters. As people move, it is likely they are improving their conditions, which they should know and understand better than strangers.

Preventing higher density projects from being built paradoxically will by limiting competition, ensure the maintenance and support of the far worse ones already in existence.

Housing Quotas

Those once despised quotas continue to appear in more fields. Housing is beginning to feel their impact. There, too, they will operate unwisely and unfairly.

Some localities are requiring builders to allocate a percentage of their developments for low- and moderate-income families, usually about 15 percent. Due to high costs of new construction, these units will have to be built with government subsidies.

In spite of all the hullaballoo, the imposition of these quotas can have no more than token consequences since they will affect comparatively few. At current prices, the spending of billions would have little impact. It would cost almost a billion dollars to produce 30,000 to 35,000 fully subsidized housing units.

Many builders resist quotas because they are risky and costly. Previous experience suggests a considerable number of subsidized units will not be financially successful, creating problems for everyone involved (including taxpayers). Investors accordingly will hesitate to undertake projects with required quotas, or seek higher profits to compensate for the added risk. Either alternative is repugnant in this day of low-housing production and inflation.

While it might appear that new conventional housing helps only the rich and subsidized construction the poor, this is not the case. On the contrary, conventional units will provide more housing opportunities than subsidized ones. Consequently, housing conditions are harmed more than helped by quotas that substitute subsidized for conventional housing. Given the choice, the latter is by far to be preferred.

The basis for this conclusion comes from analysis of how the housing market operates. Whenever a new house or apartment is built and occupied, a series of relocations are triggered, beginning with the family that moves into it. The quarters vacated by this latter family will be occupied by another that in turn vacated its residence. This process, filtration, continues down the housing ladder, as clearly disclosed in the study by the Survey Research Center of the University of Michigan.[8] This study found that on the average, 3.5 relocations occurred when a new home or apartment was occupied, and over one-third of those who moved were in the low- and moderate-income categories. Not all new housing produces the same number of moves, however. As a general rule, higher cost housing induces more moves than lower cost construction. For example, the production of a new house with a value at the time of the survey of less than $15,000 caused 2.19 moves to occur while one having a value of $25,000 to $35,000 created 3.82 moves. The figure for rental units was 1.68 relocations when the rent was less than $100 monthly and 3.16 if $200 or more.

In the case of subsidized housing, families that occupy these units frequently move from blighted quarters that may then be demolished. Often they leave a shared dwelling. Probably no more than a fraction of one move in addition to their own can be anticipated, and then only by someone still lower in the economic scale.

The construction of a nonsubsidized unit will serve more housing consumers. About one and a fraction moves can also be expected, on the basis of the survey, by people with low and moderate incomes. In addition, however, nearly the same number of moves may be anticipated of average income families who are not eligible for subsidies and cannot afford new housing. Whatever relocations are created by subsidized construction will not benefit this latter group.

These quotas will create peculiar priorities. Zoning regulations, by raising the prices of homes or banning inexpensive apartments and town houses, will exclude many average income people from a community who otherwise could afford to move there. Their taxes, however, will pay for the subsidies and enable another group, those favored by the quotas, to live in that community.

Adding insult to injury, the quotas can be a means to intensify zoning restrictions. Localities may be able to withstand judicial attack against highly exclusionary zoning by showing that they are allowing the entry of poor people. Courts have used this test in upholding zoning ordinances. Strangely, by permitting erection of a relatively few subsidized ones, the production of many more units can be prevented.[9]

Notes

1. Thomas v. Collins, 323 U.S. 516, 530 (1945).

2. R. H. Coase, *The Market for Goods and Market for Ideas,* 64 AMER. ECON. REV. 384 (1974).

3. *In re* Appeal of Kit-Mar Builders, Inc. 268 A. 2d 765 (1970).

4. LANSING, CLIFTON AND MORGAN, NEW HOMES AND POOR PEOPLE: A STUDY OF THE CHAIN OF MOVES (Ann Arbor: U. of Mich. 1969).

5. U.S. NATIONAL COMMISSION ON URBAN PROBLEMS, BUILDING THE AMERICAN CITY 266 (U.S. Gov't. Printing Office 1969).

6. JACOBS, THE DEATH AND LIFE OF GREAT AMERICAN CITIES 8-11 (N.Y: Randon House 1961).

7. CONGRESSIONAL RECORD, Oct. 21, 1971, at E11122.

8. NEW HOMES AND POOR PEOPLE, note 4 *supra*.

9. See discussion of Petaluma in chapter 5.

3 **The Case Against Zoning**

The Housing Crisis

Is any major industry as plagued with adversity as housing? In recent years catastrophe has struck it twice: first, in the guise of the environmental movement, and subsequently through the credit crunch. Then there are all the minor calamities in the form of severer zoning, construction, platting, and subdivision regulations.

Lately, the news media has finally begun to note that the current plight of the industry is also that of the average American who wants a better home. This had been forgotten by much of the press as its attention concentrated on schemes for stopping or controlling growth. For the past several years the stories about housing concentrated on the means used to curb it. Somehow the writers failed to grasp the obvious threat of the antigrowth policies, that they could succeed only at the expense of new housing. The nation's biggest postwar housing slump may change this attitude—at least for its duration. Housing starts are off substantially, and at long last, a flood of stories have been appearing describing the human problems caused by the unavailability of new housing.

Before the slump zoning was the chief obstacle to more housing construction, and it operated to deny homes and apartments to many people who could otherwise have acquired them. Like the previous economic downturns, this one also will end some day, and it will indeed be tragic if the land use controls then in force prevent the builders from making up for lost time. This latter possibility is quite likely to occur inasmuch as the housing slump will not deter many communities from passing more restrictive regulations. On the contrary, they will have an easier time of it since developers will be sidelined by their more pressing problems.

Existing residents will then continue acting as they have since the advent of zoning. Many of those fortunate enough to live in the community already, upon discovering that zoning ordinances can be used to screen housing and other developments, will do what comes naturally. They will use these laws to their own advantage; they will seek to exclude the housing, people, and commercial projects they do not want.

Since selfishness as such is not an accepted legal right, a variety of noble sounding excuses have been created to justify exclusion and make it publicly acceptable. These readily collapse upon examination. Thus, to preserve property rights of home owners, those of land owners have been sacrificed. Although the emphasis is always on increasing local revenues, apartment, commercial, and industrial projects that would augment tax collections have been barred. In the name of sound planning, local legislators have hired only those planners who shared their own views. And in pursuit of home rule, localities have adopted policies that have strongly influenced actions and events in other places.

In the middle 1960s, after more than forty years of zoning, academics and intellectuals finally caught on. They filled the scholarly journals with condemnations of local land use policies. Their catch phrase, "exclusionary zoning," became part of the language. Had these efforts continued unabated, it is likely that a great many courts would have responded by severely limiting municipal zoning powers over housing. Courts in Pennsylvania, New Jersey, Virginia and Michigan did just that.

However, as the crescendo became loudest, a saviour in the form of the environmental movement arrived. In effect, the environmentalists agreed to the facts of the indictment, but pleaded a form of self-defense. Ever stricter regulation at all levels of government, they maintained, were necessary to save and preserve the environment.

From the negative of exclusion, it became the positive of environmental protection. Whereas formerly the argument was about the kind of project that should be permitted, it now often became a question whether there should be any development at all. The use of land for trees, animals, and lagoons frequently was on a par with the use of that property to house and provide necessities for human beings.

As the years have passed, zoning has grown more and more restrictive. The drafters of the original zoning codes would gasp in horror at the current ones. That trend should be totally reversed, for if allowed to continue, it will keep us in a perpetual housing crisis.

By popular legend, zoning was established to solve problems of land use and development, but it has created greater problems. When zoning restricts the operation of the real estate market, it also restricts the supply of housing, denying more, better, and less costly housing. When zoning limits supply, it denies consumers the benefits of competition. When zoning curtails development, it curtails business activity and tax revenues.

Consider the social and economic problems zoning creates:

1. It excludes housing and people.
2. It impedes the "filtering" process.
3. It raises prices of land and property.
4. It curtails development.
5. It retards competition.

The first of these problems concerns "exclusionary zoning," which usually refers to zoning restrictions that operate to exclude the poor and near poor from suburban areas. In fact, however, all zoning is exclusionary; that is its purpose and intent. Zoning was created to exclude from communities that which is undesirable, incompatible, and adverse.

Who decides these questions? Generally the politically active and vocal people who already live in the community—those fortunate enough to have gotten there first. They control the political process, which in turn controls the zoning process. As a result of acting in their self-interests, zoning walls have been erected throughout the country that exclude portions of the population from many suburbs and more desirable sections of cities.

Impact of Zoning Restrictions

Regulation: Helping the Rich

The notion that we need governmental regulation to prevent the rich from exploiting the poor is at the basis of many laws. It happens to be wrong; frequently regulation benefits the rich much more than the poor.

Fifty years of zoning experience in the United States supports this conclusion. Zoning is one of our most pervasive forms of regulation, and its effects are by now apparent and beyond conjecture.

They show that instead of providing for the public welfare, it has done well for the private welfare of the well-to-do. It has generally been harmful to those of average and less income. The most notable exceptions, it seems, are the fortunate ones who become politicians and planners controlling zoning. If they do not become rich, at least they become powerful.

This is how zoning has discriminated against the less affluent persons in our society:

1. The best means for lowering the cost of housing, both new and existing, is to increase the supply. Zoning does exactly the reverse. It restricts the production and supply of real estate from housing to stores. Hardest hit, as a result, are those with the least money.

2. Most affluent suburban and rural communities erect zoning barriers to exclude apartments and town houses. When apartments are permitted, they usually have to comply with rigorous "snob" construction and design standards that make them affordable only by the wealthy. Their practices with respect to mobile homes are worse. These units catering frequently to families that would otherwise seek government housing subsidies are excluded from vast portions of this country.

3. Typically, those communities also do not want inexpensive homes in their midst. So they require, among other things, large lots or large amounts of interior space per dwelling, both of which add to the bill.

4. The practical operation of zoning raises development costs that are passed on to the consumer. When the local authorities rezone property for single- or multiple-family purposes, they are likely to extract conditions, legal and sometimes extra-legal, that can be quite expensive. The installation and maintenance of swimming pools and recreational facilities, for example, add significantly to the cost of housing. One of the motives behind these practices is to keep out projects that attract people of lower incomes.

5. When zoning prevents construction of new homes or apartments, it also prevents the succession of moves set in motion by that new construction—the *filtering process*. The addition of one new housing unit to the market serves not only its initial occupants, but also several other families or individuals who are able to move to other and presumably better accommodations as a result. Consequently, the exclusionary effects of zoning do not terminate at the boundary lines of a municipality, but continue on throughout the

housing market of which it is a part. The University of Michigan study of filtration shows quite clearly that one of the best means for improving housing conditions for inner city residents is through the construction of homes and apartments for the more affluent in the outlying areas.[1]

6. Zoning prohibitions tend to curtail the construction of stores and repair shops within walking or short distances of homes and apartments. In areas lacking public transportation, this creates inconvenience and hardship for a family without a car or with only an older one, particularly if it is used by the husband during the day. The rise in gasoline prices adds to the problems.

7. Zoning is harmful to the interests of small builders. There are now so many zoning rules and regulations that it requires the services of lawyers and sometimes planners and other experts to process almost any changes. Moreover, obtaining zoning approval may take months or years and that involves the expense of holding or optioning property. These conditions are eliminating small builders to the advantage of the large ones who are in a much better position to cope.

Snob Zoning

Large lot requirements have been widely blasted as "snob zoning," a device foisted by the wealthy to keep housing prices up and the less well-to-do out. A survey in the late 1960s by a Presidential (Douglas) commission[2] showed that 25 percent of metropolitan area municipalities with a population of 5,000 or more permitted no less than one-half acre lots (an acre is 43,560 square feet). In some areas, three to five acres were required. Since average priced houses seldom exceed 1,500 to 1,800 square feet, a family can live quite comfortably on much less than 22,000 square feet of ground.

This attack on large lot zoning was muted with the arrival of the environmental and stop-growth movements. More land was frequently urged for each unit of housing. "Downzoning," which involves exactly that, has, as a result, become a favorite sport of zoners. Snobbishness obviously is not the only attraction. Many want to maintain low populated areas with less congestion and more greenery and open space.

The cost of such luxury, however, may now be prohibitive in

these days of high inflation and shortages. Bigger lots require more pavement, sidewalks, curbs, gutters, lighting, water and sewer mains, and gas and electric lines. Costs across the nation for installing these improvements appear to range, depending on terrain and quantity, from $50 to $80 per front foot of lot, or roughly from $1,200 to $2,000 for each twenty-five feet of frontage.

Bigger lots will have more areas for grass and landscaping, requiring greater use of water and larger municipal facilities to provide it. Bigger lots waste land. More use of land for urban development comes at the expense of alternative uses such as farming and grazing. Large lots cause greater sprawl, which lengthens the driving distances between homes, work, and shopping, adding to our pollution problems. More gas and oil are consumed and cars depreciate faster. Greater spread increases transportation expenses of police, fire departments, and schools.

Experience shows that the problem will not be cured by "better planning and zoning." As they have in the past, most local residents will inevitably find it in their self-interest to keep housing sites large and expensive and apartment development (the best land conservers) minimal.

We all desire to live and raise our children under the most optimum conditions possible and will tend to resolve any doubts in favor of that objective. In such highly personal matters, one can seldom give equal or adequate consideration to the interests of those who would like to move into the community. Few can refrain from being judges in their own cause.

There is accordingly less urban waste in areas like Houston that are not zoned, and local residents do not exercise the same powers.

Consider just one illustration: If Houston had adopted the proposed zoning ordinance rejected by its voters in 1962, the average density of multifamily developments would have been reduced. It would have required over 7.5 instead of about 6 square miles to provide for the 100,000 apartments constructed during the following ten-year period.

Not even the most determined controllers could reasonably suggest that, as a consequence, the living conditions of the tenants have suffered. The absence of zoning has also conserved much land that otherwise would have been used up for homes and commercial and industrial purposes.

Another possible means of curbing large lot zoning is through the adoption of state or federal land use regulations. This solution, however, would be harmful to those who prefer more land than the controllers deem best. Eliminating zoning would settle the controversy within a framework of maximum freedom.

*Effect of Zoning on Living Conditions and Real
Estate Values*

But won't a glue factory be erected next to my home? That kind of fear is frequently aroused by suggestions that zoning is unnecessary and should be eliminated. The likelihood of a glue factory in a residential area without zoning is virtually nil.

There is a natural organization in urban development that tends to separate industrial and commercial uses from homes. This is not just theory; it is probably true for cities throughout the world. The land use maps of five major Texas cities that are not zoned confirm this.[3] These are the maps that show by color or other code the location of homes, apartments, commerce, and industry. They indicate that in nonzoned Houston, Pasadena, Wichita Falls, Laredo, and Baytown, industry has largely separated itself. They also show that the vast bulk of businesses are on heavily traveled, not residential streets. There are exceptions to this pattern, but probably little or no more than might occur under zoning. It is difficult to detect from maps if there is any more scattering of industry in Houston than in long zoned Dallas and Los Angeles, two cities with which Houston is popularly compared. Nor do the land use maps of zoned Amarillo, Lubbock, and Abilene, Texas look appreciably different than those of their nonzoned counterparts.[4]

Consider Baytown, Texas, population approaching 50,000, a city that has never adopted zoning. Voters defeated a proposed zoning ordinance there in 1969 by more than two to one. Baytown has some of the heaviest industry in the state as well as subdivisions containing homes valued in excess of $50,000 to $100,000. There is a clear separation between these areas. When one visits the heavy industrial area in that city, it is hard to believe that expensive homes exist a short distance away, and a similar reaction about industry occurs in the residential sections. These subdivisions have been built with due consideration for potential problems. Thus, developers made allowance for prevailing wind patterns to avoid odors and fumes from industry.

My conclusion on the basis of many discussions with industrial realtors is that their clients are about as anxious to avoid locating near homes as home owners are to avoid locating near factories. The proximity of home owners can create serious problems. Residents may complain about heavy traffic, late working hours, noise, smells—even when they do not exist.

It is near certain that no one would erect a smelly glue factory in a residential subdivision. Most subdivisions in nonzoned areas are protected by restrictive covenants (deed restrictions) against uses other than homes. Moreover, land in residential areas is usually much too costly for heavy industrial use. There is the strong probability that the factory would be shut down by nuisance laws to which development everywhere is subject. Legal expenses would be exceedingly high to fend off irate neighbors and the municipality. And there would be the serious risk that some hostile residents might vandalize the property. In short, land use maps correctly suggest that the real estate market without zoning does not operate chaotically or haphazardly; it is quite orderly.

Take the case of another pariah, gas stations. In Houston, each oil company has had the choice of purchasing for gas station construction a corner lot on a quiet residential street (not subject, of course, to deed restrictions) for a price of, say, $10,000, or of purchasing a site on a busy thoroughfare one block away for from $50,000 to $100,000. Invariably, in spite of the great price difference, the major thoroughfare lot is selected. Any other choice would be a waste of money. Success for that business demands the heavy traffic available only on major arteries. Other major businesses likewise seek high traffic and easy access. Industry wants to be near transportation facilities and expressway intersections. Houston shows that when apartment developers have free choice, they prefer certain areas. Consequently, there is less scattering of apartments in Houston than in Dallas where politicians and planners have great influence over the location.

These market forces provide considerable protection for home owners. Added security is afforded by restrictive covenants that either builders or home owners can and do impose. Houston and other nonzoned localities show that little more is needed to protect the values and reasonable desires of home owners.

Downzoning and Other Controls

The original and, for many, still major justification for zoning is that it will preserve and protect property. But examples keep multiplying of how zoning is pouring property rights down the drain.

Consider the facts of a case involving Von's Grocery Co., a leading supermart chain in California. In 1966 it and another investor, HFH, agreed to buy 5.8 acres at a major intersection in Cerritos, California, provided that the property was rezoned for commercial use to permit the development of a shopping center. It was then zoned for agricultural purposes. The city reclassified the property as requested, and Von's and HFH, in reliance on the new zoning, purchased the property for $388,000. In 1971 the city began to change its mind about this zoning. Although the other three corners of the intersection were either classified or used for commercial purposes, Cerritos in 1972 downzoned Von's property to low-density, single-family residential. The owners filed suit, claiming that the rezoning had reduced the land's value from $400,000 to $75,000. They sought payment of the difference from the city. A lower court rejected the claim, but was reversed by a 2 to 1 decision of an appellate court that the city would be liable for whatever diminution in value could be proved.[5] The dissenting judge argued that the only remedy to correct wrongful zoning was to overturn it, and that localities could not be forced to pay damages. The case has been appealed to the California Supreme Court.

What had occurred in that situation was comparable to much that is now taking place in California and the rest of the country: downzoning. Strange as it may seem, there is a mood afoot in the nation that land should remain underdeveloped, that is, utilized for less than its potential. The preferred use is low density, single family (and, of course, open space), and anything zoned otherwise is in peril of being downzoned.

Montgomery County, Maryland, which lies north of the nation's capital and its ever increasing demands on the housing market, rezoned approximately one-third of its entire land area to require a minimum lot size of at least five acres. Many owners discovered, as a result, that their land was worth much less.

This process can cause enormous losses. A land owner has filed suit for $15 million against Palo Alto, California, alleging that these are the damages it sustained when the city downzoned 500 acres from a category allowing a variety of uses, including commercial, to a highly restricted one permitting only a single house on ten acres.

Downzoning usually affects only certain parcels. A more general problem for property owners occurs when another popular obsession, growth control, is adopted by a locality. The value of most residentially zoned land is affected.

The stronger the growth controls, the greater the effect on vacant land within a locality. If, for instance, all new construction is forbidden, the value of land attributable to potential use for development purposes will largely disappear. Values will be determined by alternative uses such as farming or grazing. A one acre lot having a value of from $20,000 to $50,000 for residential purposes might be reduced in price to a fraction of that amount.

Growth controls have the effect of reducing demand, and since supply remains the same, the price of land will fall. Thus, if in a community the construction rate is about 1,000 units per year and controls limit it to 300, there will be far less demand for land with a decrease in its price. Because the supply of housing is also reduced, however, the cost of houses will rise, offsetting the land price reduction.

The manner of implementing growth controls will also influence prices for individual parcels. Petaluma, California limited the annual number of permits for development housing to about 500. Parcels selected to fill this quota may sell for a considerable amount whereas those not included will have minimal prices. The selection process will confer value.

An intrinsic condition of a free market economy is that the impersonal forces of supply and demand will determine property values. Zoning seriously wounds that system and quota type growth controls finishes it off.

Development Transfer Rights

One of the causes of the day is that of preserving buildings that have special significance, those considered cultural "landmarks." Newspapers once carried photos of Jacqueline Kennedy Onassis "picketing" Grand Central Station in New York to prevent its replacement with a high rise. Throughout the country, many other people are seeking to save historically important structures.

Frequently, however, there is a very big catch to such desires. Someone owns these buildings and the sites may have much greater value for redevelopment purposes than retained for their present use.

Most owners have no objections to preserving the structures provided they are compensated for the losses they incur in operating old buildings and in being denied the opportunity to use or sell the property for redevelopment. Few are willing or financially able to preserve history out of their own pocketbook. Nor is it fair to require anyone to carry such a financial burden for the benefit of the entire community.

The courts tend to agree. They may require the city or town to pay the owner market price for the property if it prevents demolition. Otherwise, there would be a violation of the taking clauses of the United States and state constitutions that prohibit private property from being taken for public use without just compensation. Localities have similar difficulties when they seek to preserve as open space land that is privately owned.

In spite of all the evidence that there are no free lunches, some imaginative people have dreamed up an idea that they think will provide the public with what it wants and yet compensate the owners fully. It is generally referred to as Development Rights Transfer (DRT) and is currently one of the most discussed ideas in zoning.

Under this plan, the owner of a heritage building would be given compensation for the full value of its redevelopment potential in the form of development rights that could be transferred to another site to increase the latter's zoning density. For example, land on which a one-story historical building stands has long been zoned to allow the erection of a thirty-story high rise. Under the DRT concept, the owner would be given zoning elsewhere for perhaps an additional twenty-nine or thirty stories, and would not be allowed to demolish the old building, which would thereafter be preserved (and some tax relief possibly provided to help operate it).

Proponents of DRT deserve applause for endeavoring to protect property rights. Far too many persons consider such rights merely an obstacle to "better zoning." Unfortunately, thereafter the idea bogs down. It becomes another zoning scheme with the same basic scenario as others. The public, planners, and politicians again will be making the decisions but these may be more troublesome than the usual ones.

Public officials or commissions they appoint will recommend the buildings for preservation. They will also have to decide the value of what is being transferred so that the owner will not get a zoning windfall or disadvantage at the new site. Owners with friends at the helm may suddenly be competing for, instead of avoiding such designations for their buildings. The reverse situation of communities trying to shortchange owners would be just as likely to occur.

Even greater problems will arise when the zoners decide where the rights should be transferred. Special zoning districts will have to be created and carefully restricted; else high rises might be appearing in the midst of homes. Densities in these districts will have to be reduced in anticipation of more intensive use when rights are transferred. How much will density have to be lowered? Whose property values will be sacrificed? How will owners, tenants, and mortgage lenders be protected against high rises popping up next door? Comparable dilemmas have existed since zoning began, and the public process, where political pressures are predominant, is not suited for solving them fairly or efficiently.

If special districts are not created, a DRT plan would probably be illegal. In 1972 New York City officials transferred high rise development rights without following procedures required to rezone property, such as public hearings. A court nullified the action on the ground it violated the rights to voice objections by owners and tenants in the vicinity of the transfer site.[5]

DRT would further complicate an already overly complicated situation.

Zoning and Inflation

One way to fight inflation is to do away with zoning. Zoning operates to limit construction of real estate. The immutable law of supply and demand tells us that the fewer homes and apartments in existence, the higher will be their prices. Builders and developers cannot earn money unless they build and develop. There can hardly be a stronger incentive, and it will result in the greatest amount of production practicable under the conditions that exist at any particular period. Zoning restricts this process by decreeing where and how much can be built. The consequences have been particularly evident in suburban areas where land use regulations have severely limited multi-family construction.

In numerous cities within recent years, zoning curbs have also curtailed single-family development as part of slow growth efforts. Limitations on apartments are much more common. The effects can be observed from the experience of nonzoned Houston. A proposed zoning ordinance was submitted to that city's electorate in 1962 and defeated by 57 to 43 percent. Among other things, the proposed ordinance would have prohibited construction of apartments in a great many areas where it subsequently occurred, and would, through density curbs, have reduced the number of units that could have been erected on many sites. To build multiple-family structures in places not authorized by the ordinance would have necessitated rezoning, and this frequently is refused by the authorities.

When it is granted, expensive conditions, legal and perhaps extra-legal, may be exacted that would be reflected in higher rents. Special improvements, dedications for parks and open space, and changes in design and construction may be required. Cuts in site density are also likely to raise costs. The construction cost of an individual apartment is usually greater in a smaller than a larger building.

Another way of saving money is to increase the amount of commercial and industrial development. Both produce substantially greater tax revenues than houses.

One among many examples stands out: It is the story of Greenway Plaza, which will soon be one of Houston's major commercial complexes. As of 1968 it consisted of a fifty-five-acre high rise commercial development. In that and the following year, Greenway's developer purchased almost all of the 237 homes and one apartment building in two adjacent subdivisions. To induce everyone to sell, Greenway made a generous offer. Home owners would be paid a price above market, and given five years of rent-free occupancy.

Since there were few governmental barriers that had to be overcome, the major problem confronted by the developer was buying piecemeal the two subdivisions from the many home owners. He obtained from each owner willing to sell an option for the period needed to determine if everyone else would also sell. If the property had been zoned, it would have been classified as single family and the time required to determine the city's pleasure would have lengthened the option period substantially. Not many owners would have allowed their porperty to be bound legally for the many additional months or years (or lifetime?) needed by the City Council to arrive at such an important zoning decision. This would have dissuaded a developer from undertaking such a project.

The total cost of new construction in the two subdivisions is now estimated at about $1 billion. This amount of building will generate an annual real estate tax obligation in excess of $9 million. Taxes on the land will add to this amount. Total yearly taxes on the homes and one apartment building in both subdivisions were under $125,000. The difference is enough to purchase many school rooms, parks, and open space—or, alternatively, simply to reduce taxes.

The site of the complex is close to two expressway intersections and is a short ride from downtown Houston, obviously ideal for the development contemplated. It would in all likelihood have been financially unfeasible to substitute a site with similar potential. Most of the benefits that will accrue, consequently, would have been lost under zoning.

Although Houston until 1975 was the nation's sixth largest city, it is no wonder that since 1960 it has ranked third or fourth in volume of construction, with rents among the lowest for any major city in the country. (Houston became the fifth largest city in 1975).

The Question of Nonzoning

People have said that zoning laws will never be repealed in this country, making efforts toward that end futile. However, consider the changes in attitude evident in recent years among legal scholars: Most major law journals have had articles strongly critical of zoning, some asserting that much if not all zoning is unconstitutional. Some courts are reconsidering the issue. Recent decisions in New Jersey reflect great changes in judicial thinking in that state and probably others regarding zoning: the *Township of Madison*[7] and *Township of Mount Laurel*[8] cases, which invalidated entire zoning ordinances because they excluded middle- or lesser-income housing, and the *Borough of Glassboro*[9] case, which invalidated certain restrictions on development of multifamily dwellings. The provisions and practices nullified in these cases were not unusually restrictive by today's standards. New Jersey's dubious distinction in zoning law in the past resulted from two highly exclusionary decisions. In 1952 the court upheld a minimum floor area restriction for single-family dwellings,[10] and in 1962 validated total exclusion of trailer camps within a local government.[11] Such decisions would be unlikely today in New Jersey as well as in many other jurisdictions.

Although it may come as a surprise to many, it is a fact that zoning has often done poorly in local straw votes and referendums. Some results are reported in the section that follows. Accordingly, those who are unhappy with zoning might consider subjecting the question to a referendum instead of allowing the issue to be decided in effect by what may well be a minority.

Those who cannot conceive of the abolition of zoning ought to consider the efforts of the Ford administration toward deregulation of industry. Who would ever have imagined deregulation of the airlines? The President proposed in the fall of 1975 a program toward that general end, within specified limits and stages. Its objective is to let competition, not bureaucrats dominate the airline industry. Newspapers report that the Senate Subcommittee of Administrative Practice and Procedure, chaired by Senator Edward Kennedy of Massachusetts, issued a draft report favorable to airline deregulation. The many criticisms being made in Washington of the federal regulatory agencies apply frequently to the zoning system presently operative in this country. It may be no less vulnerable.

Is nonzoning feasible and desirable for all communities, including those where land is scarce? I believe so. For example, consider the last forty acres of vacant land remaining in a community where all other land has been fully developed. The decision as to how this last vacant tract will be used in a zoned area will be made through the political processes of local government. The governing body will zone or rezone the property after hearing from all interested parties, their planners, lawyers, and other representatives. Each side will have no difficulty in producing a planner to prove "conclusively" that its position is the only correct one.

The outcome will hinge on which group is best able to influence the governing unit. Existing strong demand for apartments in the community would most likely be a much less important factor than opposition to such use by some politicians or a home owners' group. The decision is likely to be controlled by a host of factors and forces that have virtually no relationship to maximizing production, satisfying consumer demands, maintaining property rights or values, or planning soundly. A similar outcome can be expected if some land use control decisions are removed to the state or federal level, except for a change in characters and pressures.

By contrast, a land use decision where there is no zoning will be more rational. The property will likely be used in accordance with market demands, which means that directly or indirectly it will be used to satisfy the predominant consumer demand. The more a developer or his successor in ownership succeeds in supplying consumers' demands, the greater his profits are likely to be.

This is the highest and best use of the property as determined by what appears to be the *least* fallible of city planners: the marketplace. Property values will be maximized for the site in question. A location consistent with maximizing profits is also likely to be consistent with the maintenance of nearby property values. More things and more accommodations will be provided for more people. Business and community finances will benefit. And the precious land will be used productively—not wasted for the sake of planners' speculations and political expediencies.

Experience has shown that the politicians who control zoning tend to know little about land use and development, and are motivated largely by political or possibly material considerations. To entrust this group or any other group of politicians or their subordinates with substantial powers over land use is inconsistent with reason and common sense.

Zoning Elections

It is clear that not everyone equates zoning with motherhood. In November 1974, for example, the voters in two rural counties of Illinois rejected by substantial margins the adoption of zoning ordinances. At the time the vote was held, neither county had ever passed zoning.

Although there have been similar results in the past, these actions are noteworthy because they come at a time when, increasingly, we are being told that a new mood has emerged in the nation, demanding severe regulation of land use. The people have become environmentally aware—so goes the line—and will no longer tolerate "selfish abuse" of the land. The selfishness and abusiveness referred to (of course) is that of private owners, not of politicians, administrators, planners, or other citizens.

Apparently 71 percent of those voting on the question in Bond County, Illinois (population 10,000) and 60 percent in Jersey County, Illinois (19,000) do not agree. These are the figures by which zoning was defeated. Judging from prior voting results in other and larger rural counties, it is doubtful that the vote would have been much different in the "unaware" days.

A very hotly contested zoning election held in March 1972 in Escambia County, Florida (205,000) tends to confirm this conclusion. About every conceivable issue was raised, including the environmental ones, since a portion of the county is located on the Gulf of Mexico. But to no avail, for the voters refused, 64 to 36 percent, to accept zoning—this, in spite of the vehemence with which it was supported by three of the five members of the County Board of Supervisors and the principal daily newspaper.

Many advisory elections and referendums on adopting zoning in unzoned areas have been held over the years throughout the country, but no one seems to have compiled a reasonably complete list. None of the major cities except Houston, Texas ever voted on it. Most elections have been held by counties and rural townships. The only city elections that have come to my attention were held in Texas. Houston in straw votes twice voted against it, in 1947 and 1962. The margin was 57 to 43 percent in the latter year. Zoning lost three out of four contests in Wichita Falls (100,000). An overwhelming 82 percent opposed it in the last election held in 1963. In 1969 voters of Baytown (45,000) turned down zoning by 68 percent. Beaumont adopted it in 1954, although 70 percent disapproved in 1948.

Prior to the vote in Escambia, nineteen Florida counties had held thirty-one separate votes on adopting zoning, of which eighteen were unfavorable. One county held five and two counties, four votes before zoning finally won. As a result, after repeated elections, zoning was imposed in ten of these counties.

Zoning was overwhelmingly defeated in one Oregon county in 1967 and in two Iowa counties in 1968. In Ohio, as of the close of 1971, voters had defeated zoning in fifty-seven townships and approved it in eighteen. An effort to repeal zoning in Clatsop County, Oregon in 1968 lost by less than 2 percent. In many instances, such as in Escambia and Clatsop, residents of zoned cities within the counties were allowed to vote, although they would not be directly affected by the outcome. Their participation reduced the sizes of the antizoning vote and, in the case of Clatsop, caused its defeat.

Missouri appears to have held the most county zoning elections. As of 1974, twenty-two counties had voted zoning in and never voted it out, whereas seventeen had voted against or repealed it. Perhaps most interesting is that in four counties, the voters originally supported zoning, and subsequently, in 1968 and 1970, rescinded it.

There is a pattern in the 1962 Houston zoning election that appears to explain why people vote as they do; it is based on income level. The same pattern prevails in the other election returns I have analyzed, those of Baytown, Wichita Falls (1963), and Escambia. In these localities, the less wealthy voted against and the richer for zoning. In Houston, for instance, in the poorest section, more than 84 percent opposed it, in contrast to the more than 60 percent approving it in the wealthiest areas. The well-to-do came out in much larger percentages to vote, but could not overcome the greater margins that prevailed in the poorer sections.

For those who are better off, zoning is a luxury. In its absence, reasonable protection of their urban environment can be accomplished through restrictive covenants and a limited number of laws, as occurs in the nonzoned areas. The considerations are different for those of lesser means. When zoning excludes local shops, restricts construction, or raises housing costs, it creates barriers to a better life for these people. Evidently they are quite aware of the problem.

Freedom and Property Rights

Voters in Jefferson County, Missouri (pop. 110,000) have twice rejected zoning. In 1970, 56 percent voted to terminate it and 58 percent voted in 1974 against establishing county planning.

One strong opponent began his campaign shortly after discharge from the army. He purchased about an acre of land in a rural area to build a home, but was denied a building permit because the parcel was too small to qualify under the zoning ordinance. He was outraged since it was inconceivable to him that anyone could possibly have been harmed by his proposed structure.

When my learned friends hear this story, they generally react with a polite tolerance, a kind of inward yawn; so what else is new? This attitude, regrettably, forecloses discussion and feeds on itself. We seem to have forgotten that basic liberties are at stake.

Many people appear to take it for granted that persons who own land have no inherent rights to do anything with it except what the government will allow. That notion, however, is totally inconsistent with the ideals of a free society in which people should be able to do as they please unless their acts clearly harm or interfere with the liberties of others. That is the nature of freedom. The exercise of freedom is meaningful only when it involves unpopular actions or expressions. Obviously there is never a problem in engaging in conduct everyone approves. But this infrequently occurs inasmuch as people differ greatly in interests and desires. In a free society, consequently, freedom should only be limited when its exercise actually diminishes someone else's freedom; surely not when it is merely contrary to the will of a majority. By that standard, freedom in the use of property has vanished in most of this country since those who control zoning do not have to justify it on any such grounds. In fact, there is little restraint on the zoners; often they can do as they please.

Our social order has been in flux in recent years as more people who claim they have been denied them obtain "equal" rights. Personal freedom has been a critical issue of our times. Nevertheless, a reverse course has been followed on the ownership of real property. Rights of property owners have been steadily eroding due to greatly escalating zoning restrictions.

Probably the strongest support for property rights comes from the grass-roots. One can predict that in referendums affecting property interests such as those on zoning, urban renewal, or environmental restrictions, a majority of average- and moderate-income people are likely to vote against the position that restricts private property. While much of this can be explained on the basis of the harm such laws cause poorer people, these actions also stem from a belief in the riqht of the individual to freely own and use property.

This feeling differs substantially from that held by some large developers who tend to view zoning as a game of politics and expediency. Their attitude reflects the pragmatic wisdom of our times that puts property rights on the block. Many small property owners live in a less sophisticated world, and for them zoning is anything but a game; it is more a tyranny of government. However you refer to it, there is something terribly wrong when persons have to appear before local officials and plead for the opportunity to use their property as they deem best. These officials are intended to be servants, not masters, of people. Election or appointment to an office having zoning authority carries with it awesome power over other human beings. It has no place in a free society.

Zoning Proposals: More of the Same

If the substance is the same, changing the brand will not alter the effect. That, in essence, is the answer to most new schemes presently being proposed to solve the problems of zoning. They are fundamentally the same, except only for those seeking the end of zoning.

It appears that many of seemingly good intentions are hotly in pursuit of that certain special zoning system that will remove the errors and evils of the existing one. Just about everyone with any knowledge of the subject will readily acknowledge that zoning has been largely a failure and that something should be done. Still, in spite of the strong and vehement attacks planners, lawyers, and writers make, most reject scrapping it, insisting instead upon some new variety of regulation. The schemes differ in name and form, but not in substance, for the prime ingredient is still government control. Impact zoning, performance zoning, incentive zoning, zoning for quality, balanced community zoning, ecologically sensitive zoning, are some of the titles. Under each, there would supposedly be better and sounder planning, more and better housing, more open space and environmental protection, etc., all basically a repetition of rep-resentations made in the past in support of zoning, and with the same probability of success.

What the new schemes ignore is that the existence of government controls largely accounts for the problems. The same group of planners and politicians that have so dismally performed in the past are scarcely entitled to a repeat performance: Failure should not be rewarded. Politics and political expediency would remain the con-trolling factors and that spells no change whatsoever.

The terms and intent of a law are not really as important as how it is applied—and often intention and application differ radically.

When a certain zoning law clearly states one thing and many constituents insist it should be interpreted or applied differently, the politicians who must decide are certainly placed in a dilemma. Many if not most will do what is in their own best interest, and if that is contrary to the law, so be it.

The only meaningful change is to eliminate zoning and to rely on the effective and efficient forces of the marketplace to control the use and development of land and property. There will be difficulties and inequities, but much less so than presently exist and many can be met with a limited number of specific laws directed at specific problems such as, for instance, an off-street parking ordinance. The example of nonzoned Houston is available for all to observe and study the results of a different and remarkably successful approach to the regulation of land use.

The follies of zoning do not make the nightly TV news, but they are well documented in the literature, even by those favorable to the concept. Within recent years, almost every major law journal in the country has published an article highly critical of zoning practices, some, such as those appearing in the Harvard and Yale journals, contending that all or most of zoning is unconstitutional.

It is difficult to find a stronger indictment than the report made in 1968 by the professional organization of planners, the American Society of Planning Officials (ASPO), to the Presidential Commission on Urban Problems.[12] Conclusions reached in turn by that commission as well as those of two other presidential and several state commissions were equally devastating to zoning practices.

Only the termination of zoning will remove these problems.

Restrictive Covenants: Private Property Protection

Single-family living would not collapse were zoning abolished. It might well be strengthened.

If zoning were eliminated, the vast bulk of home owners who wanted to maintain single-family exclusivity would enter into restrictive covenants (often referred to as deed restrictions). These would provide a different form of control over land use but sufficient protection generally to safeguard home values and the community.

Such predictions can safely be made on the basis of the experience of nonzoned Houston, Texas. The chief means in nonzoned areas for controlling land use are restrictive covenants. In recent years, most home owners who desired this form of protection apparently have renewed or replaced the covenants when they expired. Were home owners in zoned areas faced with zoning's demise, they similarly would turn to restrictive covenants. Through this device, owners could then bind their properties to single-family use and impose other land use conditions for as long as they desired.

Restrictive covenants can contain provisions much more stringent than zoning could legally provide, and that is why they are often imposed in zoned areas. They usually govern architectural requirements, cost of construction, aesthetics, and maintenance. Being consistent with property and contract law, they are usually upheld by the courts except where they infringe on strong public policies such as those relating to racial discrimination.

For restrictive covenants to remain effective, the law requires that they be diligently enforced by the home owners. Inasmuch as this can be costly for home owners in lesser income and small subdivisions, in Houston and some other nonzoned places, the cities enforce the covenants.

Unlike zoning, covenants cannot be tampered with politically. Through the process of variations and amendments, many changes in zoning within and adjoining existing neighborhoods are annually allowed. A Presidential (Douglas) Commission concluded, on the basis of studies of three widely separated communities: Philadelphia, Pennsylvania, Alameda County, California, and Lexington, Kentucky, that "large numbers of patently illegal variances are granted each year."[13]

Houston also provides evidence that controls are not necessarily essential to keep intact a residential neighborhood. Many subdivisions in which covenants never existed or have long expired have retained their residential character. There are simply no pressures on those residential streets for anything else.

In lower income areas, all land use controls are harmful to residents. They prevent commercial facilities from locating within covenient access, making it more difficult for people of limited means to purchase necessities. Surveys of zoning elections held in various localities, invariably show that residents of those areas strongly oppose them.

In Houston's zoning straw vote of 1962, some of the poorer

sections of the city that were never subject to covenants rejected zoning by a five to one margin. Apparently they were not disturbed by the existence of a relatively limited number of commercial (5 percent to 7 percent), industrial (1 percent) and multifamily (5 percent) uses. On the contrary, the evidence is that they preferred the proximity of the commercial uses.

It is clear, however, that the more wealthy do want all the protection they can get. An article in the *Southern California Law Review* several years ago, suggested that if zoning were abolished, a government agency should be established to assist owners in preparing and executing restrictive covenants.[14] Home owners would still have the option as to whether to impose them, however.

To completely control an area by restrictive covenants where none exist requires an agreement by every owner, since only the properties of those who sign are bound. Experience in Houston shows that from 70 percent to 100 percent of home owners on residential streets in the middle- and upper-income areas will probably consent, and this for practical purposes ordinarily should be enough to exclude other uses.

These homes are either too expensive or not in demand for other uses. Consequently, in the affluent sections, agreement by as little as 70 percent could checkerboard a residential area and make it nearly as protected as 100 percent agreement.

Upon removal of zoning, home owners will no longer have power over the use of land outside of their own areas. This is a major reason for eliminating zoning. Through restrictive covenants, however, they would be able to draft controls more suited to their own local life-styles. Such local control may be far more beneficial than the centralized regulation of zoning.

Notes

1. LANSING, CLIFTON and MORGAN, NEW HOMES and POOR PEOPLE (Ann Arbor: U. of Mich. 1969).

2. U.S. NATIONAL COMMISSION ON URBAN PROBLEMS, BUILDING THE AMERICAN CITY 214 (U.S. Govt. Printing Office 1969).

3. Land use maps for Houston, Laredo and Wichita Falls were prepared by Texas Highway Commission, Austin, Texas and are

included in publications of that office. Private firms prepared the maps for Pasadena (Marmon, Mok and Green) and Baytown (Bernard Johnson Engineers).

4. Texas Highway Commission has also prepared land use maps for Dallas, Amarillo, Lubbock and Abilene.

5. H.F.H. Ltd. v. Superior Court, 41 C.A. 3d 908 (1974).

6. French Investing Company, Inc. v. City of New York, 352 N.Y.S. 2d 762 (1973).

7. Oakwood at Madison, Inc. v. Township of Madison, No. L-7502-70 P.W. (N.J. Super. Ct., Oct. 27, 1971).

8. Southern Burlington County N.A.A.C.P. v. Township of Mount Laurel, No. 25741-70 P.W. (N.J. Super. Ct., May 1, 1972). Aff'd in part by Supreme Court of New Jersey, Mar. 24, 1975, 336 A.2d 713.

9. Molino v. Mayor and Council of the Borough of Glassboro, 281 A.2d 401 (1971).

10. Lionshead Lake, Inc. v. Township of Wayne, 89 A.2d 693 (1952).

11. Vickers v. Township Committee of Gloucester Township, 181 A.2d 129 (1962).

12. U.S. Commission on Urban Problems, *Problems of Zoning and Land Use Regulation*, Research Report No. 2 (American Society of Planning Officials, 1968).

13. U.S. NATIONAL COMMISSION ON URBAN PROBLEMS, *supra* Note 2, at 226.

14. Note: *Land Use Control in Metropolitan Areas: The Failure of Zoning and a Proposed Alternative*, 45 S. CAL. L. REV. 335 (1972).

4

Consequences of Legislative Control

The Regulatory Process

A small step, little impact; a modest proposal.

These are some of the descriptions given certain national land use bills introduced in Congress. Some Congressmen who are usually vigorous opponents of increased federal powers have been persuaded that the proposed legislation will not appreciably augment the federal role in land use. They could not be more wrong. The adoption of any legislation in a field where none exists is always an act of major consequence.

Entering a room through a locked door is much more difficult than through one that is slightly ajar. Once regulatory authority has been established, it is far less of a problem to increase that power by subsequent amendments that individually may be minor but in the aggregate over the years produce major changes.

Moreover, it is becoming increasingly evident that there can be little certainty about the impact of legislation until after it has become law. Remember that modest resolution of Congress under which millions of Americans saw service in Viet Nam? That was the Tonkin Gulf resolution. It was not a declaration of war and contained only six paragraphs; few legislators who voted for it imagined that it could be used by two Presidents as authority to carry on a major war in Southeast Asia. Unfortunately, there is no way to forecast the effectiveness, cost and consequences of proposed government regulations. We learn most of these matters after, not before, controls are adopted. By then, it is too late; many vested interests have been created, and it is very difficult to do away with the laws that were passed.

It is quite simple to find problems in the country, or for that matter, of the human race. Regulatory laws are continually being passed, because their proponents keep emphasizing the problems, and ignoring or minimizing those that legislation invariably creates. Many legislators seem to operate under the assumption that the problems will automatically disappear when the laws are passed. Not only will those difficulties arise which are presently predictable but experience shows some will occur that we cannot now envision. I doubt that many original proponents of railroad or airline regulation would have believed that frequently the controls would operate to increase rather than decrease fares; or that the desire for reducing air pollution would give the EPA a reason to control the use of land; or that the regulation of pharmaceuticals would hamper the elimination of the most harmful of man's diseases; or that the regulation of natural gas production would create serious shortages of that resource. There are many other such examples. Possibly every regulation has caused in time courses of action which were never conceived of by its original supporters. Many would have voted differently had they known.

Accordingly, in evaluating the likely results of regulation, substantial allowance ought to be made for the then unknown and unpredictable consequences it will cause. But how does one introduce an unidentifiable and immeasurable factor in the debate? How can one possibly point to undesirable actions that are likely to be taken without being able to identify them? The answer is that enough is understood about regulation that this factor is not as vague as might appear.

Economics Professor Ronald Coase of the University of Chicago Law School, writes that many intensive studies have been made in the last 15 years of government regulation, more so than ever before. He is the editor of the *Journal of Law and Economics,* published by the Law School, which has printed numerous such studies and, as a consequence, he is intimately acquainted with their findings.

The studies with which he is familiar concern the regulation of many diverse activities, such as agriculture, aviation, banking, broadcasting, drugs, electricity supply, milk distribution, natural gas supply, railroads and trucking, taxicabs, whisky labeling and zoning. Says Professor Coase:

The main lesson to be drawn from these studies is clear; they all tend to suggest that the regulation is either ineffective or when it has a noticeable impact, that on balance the effect is bad, so that consumers obtain a worse product or a higher priced product or both, as a result of the legislation. Indeed, this result is found so uniformly as to create a puzzle; one would expect to find in all these studies at least some government programs that do more good than harm.[1]

Coase believes that, in theory at least, there is no reason that government regulation cannot improve on the market process, and lead to greater economic efficiency. He states, however, "[m]y puzzle is to explain why these occasions seem to be so rare, if not non-existent."[2] Professor Coase does help us with the dilemma of how to predict the results of a proposed new economic regulation. Even if we cannot supply all the details, experience is exceedingly persuasive that it will on balance operate adversely.

History likewise reveals that federal programs once begun inevitably keep growing. Once passed, there seems to be no turning back, regardless of the resultant failures. Enactment of a national land use act would mean acknowledgement of federal responsibility in the field, and seldom is such responsibility abdicated. Failures usually lead to more substantive legislation, not termination or modification of that which already exists.

Those who benefit from laws or rely on them in their businesses can be expected to lobby actively for their preservation and enlargement. For example, the strongest and most influential supporters of subsidized housing in the country at present are probably not the poor or the liberals. On the contrary, it is the National Association of Home Builders, many of whose members have benefitted substantially from the construction of subsidized housing. These builders were disturbed when the Nixon administration froze the subsidy programs; they had looked forward to a steady federal involvement. Some builders in reliance on the programs had invested in land and plans, and there is little question that they sustained harm upon curtailment of the programs.

When one considers all of the land use problems that proponents of national land use legislation have been able to conjure up, each of the proposed measures is indeed a modest one. Why then so mild a bill? Because, it is frankly acknowledged, only a modest proposal could get through Congress. The strongest proponents have made it quite clear that they will press for considerably more in the future. Hence, even before its enactment, we have already been informed of its inadequacy, and that is how it will always appear to some or many who will continually attempt to enlarge it. Theirs is the never-ending quest for that Camelot where the sun shines all day and it rains only at night. Unfortunately, in legislating toward that end, history shows that they will only create blizzards and storms for the rest of us.

Pressures on Government

One of the many difficulties in implementing a federal program, such as would be created by national land use legislation, is that, except perhaps in emergencies, representative government must necessarily respond to the continual and varied pressures and demands of its citizens. By participating and getting involved in local matters, individuals or groups, constituting small minorities can exert substantial influence, even impeding plans and efforts of the highest elected officials.

A case history of the exercise of such powers, and the ensuing problems presented government is contained in Martha Derthick's *New Towns In-Town*.[3] The book describes the efforts of President Johnson, beginning in the summer of 1967, to build housing developments for the poor in various metropolitan areas on federal surplus land. The government owned the land and the legislative authority for funding and development was then in existence. At the helm was a President personally committed to carrying out the program and willing to commit the full powers of his office toward that end. He appeared certain of success given the circumstances at hand. Nevertheless, four years after the program began, it was almost a complete failure. Of seven announced proposals for new communities, three were dead and the future of the others was in great doubt. In only one instance was a small amount of construction proceeding. The record of each of the seven proposals is basically the same. Private citizens and organizations, together with officials at various levels of government responding to the pressures of their constituents, were able to prevail over the will of the administration. (Another problem was the conflict between the different government agencies involved in planning the program and using the surplus lands.)

One of the sites was a 335 acre tract, located a few miles from the White House in Northeast Washington, D.C., which the administration initially sought to develop with 4500 units, all but 800 intended for public and subsidized housing. It was to be a showcase development in the nation's capitol, evidencing the country's concern for its less fortunate citizenry. Presumably in the federal city, the administration would have maximum influence and impact. But its powers did not extend over local officials and citizens. Strong opposition soon arose, both from neighboring residents who wanted only middle class housing and from various other persons and organizations elsewhere in the city who demanded a host of changes in the plans. A law suit was filed to obtain "meaningful" citizen participation. Virtually from the moment the program was announced, it went straight downhill; even a new school proposed for the community became the subject of controversy as to whether it should be "conventional" or "new and relevant"; and there were, of course, many opinions on that issue.

Dr. Derthick does not suggest that in any of the seven situations, there were any "bad guys" seeking personal monetary gain; almost everyone involved ostensibly desired the best use of the land, but this usually meant adopting only his own preferred plan. Basically, the forces that blocked the program reflected the national concerns of that period. Perhaps in certain places some of these particular pressures may have receded over time, but they have been or will be replaced by others; comparable ones will always be with us, as well they should in a representative and participatory society.

Recognize the scenario? It is a preview of some of what can be expected to occur upon passage of a national land use bill. This legislation will involve much more planning, regulation and commitment at all levels of government. In addition, unlike the case of surplus land, the land that will be the subject of the lobbying, jockeying and manuevering will be that of private citizens, not government owned. And infinitely more land will be involved than just seven sites. Among other things, this situation does not bode well for the rights of private ownership, since the owner will be just one of many, many divergent interests attempting to dictate its use.

Goals of National Land Use Regulation

One hears quite frequently that there must be a new attitude toward land use, that we can no longer live with the policies of the past. These words usually preface an argument favoring strong national or state land use regulation. Controls at these higher levels, it is claimed, will prevent waste and misuse of land and end urban sprawl. "It will preserve the land for generations yet unborn."

There is little substance to merit the flowery prose. The proposed controls will accomplish more of what proponents say they want to prevent. Instead of conserving a precious resource, more of it will be misused and wasted.

This point can perhaps best be explained by considering the objectives of the environmental groups advocating state and federal land use controls. They seek to carefully screen or prevent development in areas they consider "environmentally sensitive" or, as it is phrased by legislative draftsmen, "areas of critical environmental (or state) concern." They mercifully would permit development on the balance of the earth provided it is also under rigid governmental supervision.

What are areas of critical environmental concern? According to H.R. 10294, dated September 13, 1973:[4]

(a) The term "areas of critical environmental concern" means areas as defined and designated by the State on non-Federal lands, by the tribe on reservation or other tribal lands, or by the public land management agency head with respect to the Federal public lands where uncontrolled or incompatible development could result in damage to the environment, life or property, or the long-term public interest which is of more than local significance. Such areas, subject to definition as to their extent, shall include

(1) fragile or historic lands, where uncontrolled or incompatible development could result in irreversible damage to important, historic, cultural, scientific or esthetic values or natural systems which are of more than local significance, such lands to include coastal zones; significant beaches, dunes and estuaries; significant shoreland of rivers, lakes and streams; rare or valuable ecosystems and geological formations; significant wildlife habitats; scenic or historic areas; and natural areas with significant scientific and educational values;

(2) natural hazard lands, where uncontrolled or incompatible development could unreasonably endanger life and property, such lands to include flood plains and areas frequently subject to weather disasters, areas of unstable geological, ice or snow formations and areas with high seismic or volcanic activity;

(3) renewable resource lands, where uncontrolled or incompatible development which results in the loss or reduction of continued long-range productivity could endanger future water, food, and fiber requirements of more than local concern, such lands to include watershed lands, aquiter

recharge areas, significant agricultural and grazing lands and forest lands and
(4) such additional areas as are determined to be of critical environmental concern.

The language was so broad that some thought the entire state of Arizona was included, or possibly a majority of it and other Western states. However, regardless of this language or the intent of its sponsors, it is not likely that all development will or can be prohibited within these areas. What will happen in all probability is much more of what is already occurring under local zoning. There would be less development and the prices for real estate would increase. However, relatively few of the critical areas would be preserved in their natural setting.

There are two reasons for this. The more important one concerns the taking provisions of federal and state constitutions that private property shall not be taken for public use without just compensation. The second reason is that the regulatory process tends to solve controversies through some compromise formula, and this approach would be reinforced in this situation by the provisions of taking clauses. The regulators probably would seek to resolve most problems by requiring a less intensive land use. For example, instead of preventing construction of an apartment building containing 100 units on a site adjoining the ocean, the development would be allowed, but the number of apartments reduced to say, 65 to 85, with possibly an easement to the water and additional landscaping required. A slim five story building might be transformed to a squat three story one. A proposed house might have to be set back farther from the ocean, and reduced in size.

The foregoing examples describe the course generally being followed in California under its Coastal Zone Conservation Act which is intended to control development for environmental purposes within 1000 yards of the coastline. The experience under that law suggests how others of similar intent will fare. Although many changes have been required and there is increased cost, considerable delay and red tape, only a fraction of requests for development have been denied. During 1973, 6,236 permit applications were received by the six regional commissions in the state administering the act. Of this total, 5,191 were granted and 146 denied; the remainder were being processed as of the beginning of 1974.[5]

Professor M. Bruce Johnson reports that in its first fourteen months of operation, the commission he served on approved 95 percent of the applications received for single family dwellings, but granted only 60 percent of the single family units requested on these applications. While 77 percent of the multi-family applications received approval, only 51 percent of the units applied for were allowed.[6]

Results should be similar in most areas of critical environmental concern. Development would take place, but with less intensity of use and while there would be more open space, it would be privately owned and not normally accessible to the public. Even if the developer is required to provide access to a body of water, it is doubtful that many non-residents would avail themselves of the opportunity. It is even questionable that better views would be provided, since the buildings might also have to be aesthetically compromised. Some developers might try to beat the game by asking for more than they really wanted, an obvious possibility that would turn the whole process into a farce.

These restrictions would lead to increased use of land in other places to provide for the demand for housing or industry that remain unsatisfied. There might then have to be other confrontations with environmental objectives since nature, wildlife, scenic or unusual terrain, trees and lagoons might be affected in these other areas. Supply in and around the critical environmental areas would suffer, reducing competition and pushing prices upward. Similar situations might prevail throughout the general area because supply might never catch up. The consequences would be an uneconomical and wasteful utilization of land. Much more land than necessary will be utilized for urban purposes.

The Rise and Fall of National Legislation

Congress Earns Some Points

As Congress convened in January 1973, little seemed more certain than the passage of some form of national land use legislation. Its supporters were even then already devising new means to strengthen the federal presence once it had been established.

About a year later the picture had completely changed. In late

February of 1974 the House Rules Committee voted nine to four against sending a land use measure recommended by the House Interior Committee to the floor for debate and vote, and that action dimmed drastically the prospect of a national land use law for that session.

The Senate passed a similar bill in 1973, which like the House Committee's version, would have provided $800 million over the next eight years for states to develop comprehensive plans for regulating the use of land. Originally the administration had strongly backed the legislation but it, too, became disenchanted and switched support to a very mild bill. The vote of the Rules Committee and position of the administration reflected growing opposition to the legislation.

Probably the principal factor favorable to the adoption of national land use controls was the minimal knowledge the public and the communications media had about this highly complicated area. Backers touted the bill as an aid to a wide variety of popular causes, from removing unsightly hamburger stands to saving the land for future generations from the rapacious and unscrupulous developers. It was difficult to contest legislation that is supposedly preserving one of the country's most precious resources for the common interest, not allowing it to be squandered on selfish uses.

Unfortunately for its proponents, however, the selfishness issue on the Washington scene is usually a case of the pot calling the kettle black. It became apparent that the bill's principal sponsorship was from one of the most vociferous special interest groups, the environmentalists, and would be administered by another, the politicians and bureaucrats at federal and state levels. That is a combination that would invariably impede development of the land upon which much of business and labor is dependant for their livelihood.

An unusual alliance of industry and labor consequently emerged to fight the legislation and, for at least one time, the U.S. Chamber of Commerce and the carpenters' union had a common legislative objective. They successfully argued to members of Congress that the bill, by curtailing development, would further deteriorate an already bleak economic outlook. In short, they said the legislation spelled unemployment, business slowdown, and increased cost of housing.

Other factors account for the loss in support for this legislation:

First, there is great disillusionment in Congress with the performance of another bureaucracy, the Environmental Protection Agency (EPA). It has attracted environmental enthusiasts whose proposals frequently seem without basis in the laws Congress has passed. With that experience in hand, there was no forecasting what the bureaucrats would do when given authority over the vast amount of private property in the nation.

Second, the environmentalist movement appears for the moment to have lost its steam. The energy crisis has created great cynicism about the groups that stalled the Alaskan pipeline for years and now seek to stop the development of many conventional energy sources. Congress may be more willing to challenge the environmentalists' demands on the grounds that their proposals are exceedingly injurious, not beneficial, to the living environment of the average person.

Third, this legislation loomed as a serious threat to property rights. Already publications sponsored or inspired by a federal agency, the Council on Environmental Quality, complained that court interpretations of constitutional provisions on property rights were preventing government from having maximum control over the use of the land.

National Land Use Dies Again

On June 11, 1974, the House of Representatives refused by a 211 to 204 vote to consider debating and voting on two pending land use measures, thereby defeating such legislation for that session. Proponents could no longer complain that "special interests" had blocked consideration of the bill by the House.

Many headlines carried this charge after the House Rules Committee in February voted nine to four against allowing the land use measure cleared by the Interior Committee to go to the House floor. That is usually considered a mortal blow. However, recovery was swift. An understanding was reached between members of Rules and Interior, and hearings were set for the end of April before Interior. Over forty out of sixty witnesses testified against passage or in favor of scheduling regional hearings, but the committee failed to change even one comma in the bill it previously approved. Nevertheless, the Rules Committee reversed itself in May, eight to seven, and sent the measure to the floor to its second and final death.

The action of the House was a substantial setback for the environmental coalition, and cries of anguish, outrage, and nonsense poured forth. Two presidential hopefuls, Senator Jackson and Representative Udall, were principal sponsors of the measure, and they were making strange noises about, of all things, the politics of the situation.

The environmental groups, who see salvation in more and more governmental controls, were thundering against future sprawl and haphazard development, but their credibility on this issue was close to zero. Since the beginning of the so-called period of environmental awareness, there has been probably greater sprawl and waste of land than ever before. This is due partly to their success in restricting housing construction in many places, thereby forcing it further outward. Also, by demanding bigger lots and less intensive use of land, environmentalists and their allies are causing increasingly more land to be developed to house the same number of families, needlessly gobbling it up.

As the author of two provisions in the bill reported by the House Interior Committee, I might add that technically it was highly complex, with many of its important provisions ambiguous and some contradictory. Federal agencies and courts would ultimately have to decide what most of it meant. However, that is the wrong way to write laws. Congress should not decline its constitutional mandate in favor of bureaucrats and judges.

The New Mood

On July 15, 1975 the U.S. House Interior Committee killed national land use legislation for that session of Congress by a vote of twenty-three to nineteen. Several congressmen attributed defeat to intense pressure from the grass-roots, one stating that he had seldom experienced so much opposition to a bill in over a dozen years in office.

What happened to the "new mood"? That is what formed the basis for the widely distributed Final Report of the Task Force on Land Use and Urban Growth, chaired by Laurance Rockefeller and published as a book by the Rockefeller Brothers Fund.[7]

The twelve distinguished members of the Task Force found that there was a "new mood" in America that challenged the "ideal of growth" and they recommended in response, sweeping changes in laws and judicial rules that would give government close to complete dominance over the use of the land.

The report has had an unusual impact. It was of course

enthusiastically received by the environmentalists and may have increased their numbers. At the same time, however, it frightened the apathy out of a great number of persons of different persuasion. For them, the book clearly set forth a program that would eliminate their precious right to own and use land.

It was no longer a matter of conjecture; the words made it plain that certain people in high places considered the rights of property owners as an obstacle to "better" use of the land. These individual rights had to give way for the overall good. That thought precipitated active opposition from ranks that might otherwise have remained silent.

While the experience of the Task Force suggests that one should not be hasty in ascribing something like a national mood, there is much reason to believe that at present, the nation's attitude is contrary to what was depicted. The vote of the House Interior Committee supports that view. Here is some additional evidence from widely separate parts of the country:

1. On May 20, 1975, the voters of Newton County, Missouri (pop. 33,000) overwhelmingly rejected in a referendum, the adoption of zoning for their county by a margin of 6,081 to 176 (34 to 1). They also voted against instituting county land use planning, 5,917 to 219 (27 to 1). While many elections have gone against zoning, this is by far its most crushing defeat.

2. In summer of 1975, the voters of Colorado Springs, Colorado, substantially rejected two open space proposals. One would have authorized the issuance of bonds in the amount of $5 million to acquire property for this purpose. It was defeated 15,161 to 9,037 (63 to 37 percent). The other was to earmark ten percent of sales and use taxes to acquire and maintain open space. It lost 14,516 to 9,356 (61 to 39 percent).

3. Utah held a referendum in November, 1974 on a proposed land use law for the state. The vote against the measure was 242,068 and the vote for 157,438. State land use regulation was thus defeated by a 60 to 40 percent margin.

4. In spite of the 1970 enactment of preparatory legislation covering primarily larger scale development in the state, the Vermont legislature to date has refused to implement it by passing a state land use plan. The opposition since then has been so vigorous that the state planning director in 1975 advised the governor against submitting any such plan to the legislature in 1976. He said that there

had been a decline in environmental enthusiasm due to an increase in economic problems.

With the props thus undermined from their first effort, the Rockefeller Task Force ought now to prepare a sequel. They might solemnly consider whether people's rights should depend on the vagaries of the public mood.

Impact on Property Rights and Housing

National Legislation and Property Rights

One of the reasons leading to the 1974 defeat of national land use legislation was the fear that the bill would deprive people of their property rights. Nonsense, said its proponents, and they pointed to a provision in that as well as the 1975 bill that says the act shall not "enhance or diminish the rights of owners of property as provided by the Constitution of the U.S. and the constitution and laws of the states in which the property is located."

For Howard Hughes that might be comforting, but for the small land owner, it is close to meaningless. No matter how wicked, reprehensible, and confiscatory a regulation is, a bolt from heaven will not strike it dead. It can only be declared unconstitutional by a court of law, and this means that an owner must be in a position to use costly and lengthy court processes to sue for such a ruling.

The situation faced by affluent owners will be entirely different from that of the less affluent. Consider, for example, the case of wealthy and not-wealthy land owners, each confronted with a proposed harsh and probably unconstitutional regulation of their land. From the moment the regulation is even contemplated those financially able will begin employing lawyers and experts to protect their interests. They will be in a far better position to defeat or modify the proposal than those who cannot afford representation and have to represent themselves (if at all), especially where the regulators are located in the state capitol many miles away.

If the regulation is adopted, the cleavage between rich and average owners will become even greater. Before owners can obtain court rulings declaring a law unconstitutional, the following must exist or occur:

1. They must have sufficient funds to hire a lawyer to file a lawsuit against the state.

2. They must be prepared to litigate the case in the state's highest court, for if the state loses in the lower court it might appeal. The preceedings may drag on for two to three years, and they will have to spend many thousands of dollars. During this time the owner will have to continue paying taxes and possibly interest on a mortgage on the land, the amount of which may be in excess of 20 percent.

3. They must be willing to risk changing market conditions that may make their hoped for use unfeasible. Recent events provide an example: Construction that was profitable in 1971 to 1973 was frequently no longer so in 1974 and 1975. There is also risk in possibly incurring the wrath of authorities who may not look kindly in the future on those who sue them.

4. The higher court judges will have to find the law unconstitutional, and unless all commercial use of the property has been prevented, there can be little certainty as to how they will decide. It is also possible that the court may find some technical error that will cause it to dismiss the case or send it back for retrial.

Under these circumstances, even the biggest owners, builders, or developers might not consider the filing of such a lawsuit a reasonable business risk. The problem is infinitely greater for those of less means. They may have to settle for a give-away sales price or hang on to await future appreciation.

Are there not organizations prepared to help the ordinary citizen, perhaps the civil liberties groups? Hardly. For property rights would be involved and these groups seem to have read the provision safeguarding them out of the Bill of Rights. Nor, of course, would the public defender be authorized to intercede, even though an owner can lose as much in money because of government land use restrictions as he or she could from being fined for committing a crime.

The big owners and developers have the capability and will frequently defeat regulations. While the state authorities may find it difficult to overcome them, they will easily succeed against those who cannot fight back. In other words, the law in practice will do exactly the reverse of what is written and intended: It will enhance property rights for some (rich owners) and diminish those of others (average owners).

More Troubles for Housing

The construction industry in 1975 was one of the most ailing in the nation. Residential development was at the lowest ebb since World War II. Therefore, that would have been about the worst time imaginable to impose a whole new level of controls over it. Under proposed national land use legislation federal and state governments would have become part of the zoning establishment and dozens of new rules would have been added to those that now exist. Already construction is highly regulated. In most places, a nail seldom goes in without numerous governmental approvals.

The bulk of medium- and large-size projects presently require some sort of local zoning dispensation and this may require months and years to accomplish. To obtain needed zoning, a developer might have to submit the proposal to the local planning department, school and park districts, building, fire, engineering and traffic departments, environmental agencies, the planning commission, and the city council. Each one could possibly veto the application. In many states, and for certain projects, approval of state agencies would be required. If any of these bodies would demand changes, the developer probably would have to make them and resubmit the amended plans to each of the others for reapproval. It now necessitates considerable fortitude, time, and money to negotiate this obstacle course, and if difficulties should multiply, many builders and investors would look for greener pastures. Many small builders already have found that these problems are insurmountable.

The proposed national legislation, by superimposing federal and state rules, would at the very least create considerable uncertainty and confusion for owners and developers. Land use would be regulated from Washington, the state capitol, and the locality. It might be necessary to hire counsel and experts in all three places just to determine who regulates what.

The general idea behind this legislation was to remove from the control of localities those land use decisions that are considered of regional or state concern. Cities and towns would then be left to administer the matters that are of local interest.

This approach may sound simple, but is far from it. It is difficult to determine just where the local concern ends and that of the state begins. Thus, housing decisions of the suburbs mostly affect potential home owners and tenants living outside their borders. Many shopping centers and factories supply or employ far more people who live outside than within the towns where they are erected.

On this basis, many if not most local zoning powers could be removed from the localities and turned over to the state. Some authorities advocate this solution for zoning problems. This will not occur, however, because the municipalities are very powerful in the legislatures, and are not about to retire from the zoning business. The likely pulling and tugging between the local, state, and federal agencies will create much trouble for those in the middle of the power struggle: the many persons dependent for a better life on the use of the land.

The proposed national measure would have required the state to control development in "areas of critical environmental (or state) concern." Only broad definitions of this phrase were contained and much land might be frozen until the matter would be resolved by the state or the courts. The environmentalists and probably state authorities would attempt to broaden, and the developers and localities, to narrow its meaning. Lawsuits inevitably would be filed, causing the properties in question to be unavailable for use while the proceedings are pending.

The bills did seek to overcome some exclusionary zoning practices by giving the state authority over a "development of regional impact." The legislation, however, had a strong environmental orientation and that would have caused doubts to be resolved by limiting rather than increasing development. At the federal level, authority would be vested in the Interior Department, which traditionally represents conservationist interests.

Moreover, most state legislatures are suburban-rural dominated. Legislators from these areas frequently represent the same perspective as do the local politicians who adopt zoning ordinances. It is hard to believe that they would force much development against the wishes of their constituents. Thus, the New York state legislature in 1973, as a result of pressures from local governments, stripped the Urban Development Corporation, a state agency, of its powers to override local land use regulations.

The state will probably provide token recognition for the housing problems of the less affluent through some provision for subsidized housing for moderate- and low-income families. It is doubtful, however, that such tokenism will accomplish little more than to assuage the consciences of the law makers. It certainly will not serve the large numbers of people not poor enough to qualify for subsidized housing and not rich enough to afford new housing. Massachusetts enacted legislation in 1969 to overcome suburban intransigence towards subsidized housing, and its experience to date suggests that very few of those who would be eligible will ever benefit from such laws.

In short, the proposed legislation was highly unfavorable to the production of housing.

Congress as a Zoning Board

The world's biggest zoning board: that is what Congress would be if Section 503(d) of the 1975 National Land Use Bill in the House of Representatives (HR 3510) had become law. Under this provision, no rules or regulations proposed by the federal regulatory agency created by the statute would take effect until they had been submitted to Congress and not been disapproved by both houses within sixty days.

The basis for this provision is quite understandable. Regulatory agencies established by Congress have frequently flaunted the will of their creator. In setting up agencies, Congress has usually compromised between a specific, detailed description of their duties and a broad grant of power. As a result, regulatory legislation usually assigns a certain overall task to an agency and confines it with a series of generalizations, each urging in essence the accomplishment of a particular good or the avoidance of a specific evil. A majority to pass a law can be mustered on this basis in spite of the absence of a consensus on many specific policies or programs that would be undertaken by the agency. The agencies thereby end up with enormous amounts of discretion.

Section 503(d) was an attempt to avoid such problems, but it would only result in more. The Interior Department would have been charged with establishing rules and regulations under that bill, and when it did just that, some people would win and others would lose. Individuals and groups differ enormously on how the land should be used and regulated.

Not only are obvious groups such as developers and environmentalists concerned, but also farmers, labor, apartment and shopping center owners, mortgage investors, retailing companies, industrialists, utilities, tenants organizations, local and state officials, lumbermen, cattlemen, civil rights groups, mineral and mining interests, consumer organizations, etc. Many of these and their lobbyists, lawyers, and experts would descend on Washington to plead their causes. Those who did not like the contemplated rules would seek changes and those who did like them would want to make sure that they remained intact.

Congressmen would be placed in the position of land planners, deciding which of competing interests should be favored—and that at least should be an enlightening experience for them. They would then realize that there is nothing special, unique, or magical about "planning." They would know why those with the biggest political or financial clout tend to win, and why planning "solutions" depend on the opinions, tastes, perspectives, and personal interests of the decision makers.

Those who did not favor the proposed rules for certain reasons would seek out groups that disliked them for other reasons. Strange alliances would be formed, as often occurs in politics.

The goal would be to draft changes acceptable to a majority in both houses. Compromises based on political considerations would emerge, which can have little relationship to the best, wisest, efficient, or effective use of the land, that precious resource that the bill allegedly is designed to save.

In spite of its imperfections, however, Congress is about as capable of solving land use problems as any agency it sets up. Any governmental body with power over the land will operate under comparable pressures and with corresponding inclinations. Anyone with doubts on this score should examine the history of zoning in this country. There, too, a struggle has continually existed between a host of varied interests, and winners and losers are usually determined on the basis of the political pressures they can exert.

Even if a national land use bill is passed without 503(d), much the same problem will still exist for congressmen. They will be pressed continually to make changes in the legislation or to obtain favorable rulings of the agencies concerned. Whether they want to or not, they will take on duties ordinarily performed by zoning board members. So many constituents are involved in or benefit from land use that the legislators will not be able to remain aloof. Much of their time will be needlessly consumed in the process and congressmen already have too little available to pursue diligently their existing duties.

One of the problems that zoning has created is that it preempts the bulk of time of local elected officials, leaving them little left for more vital matters. It has been variously estimated that municipal councils spend 60 to 90 percent of their time on zoning. A comparable situation must not develop on Capitol Hill. Congressmen should not have to set aside consideration of bills affecting war and peace, recession and prosperity to discuss or argue with constituents about location of a factory, whether a large housing development should be allowed, or if enough open space has been provided. This is bound to occur once the federal government assumes responsibility in the use of the land.

Expedient Fallacies

Some real estate and business groups are supporting national land use legislation. Others are offering their own land use control measures at the state level. While a certain amount of this activity comes from conviction, much of it is based on expediency, trying to beat environmentalists to the punch, and a desire to promote a "progressive" image. Such people are playing with high explosives. They ought to contemplate carefully the lessons of zoning and other regulatory controls.

The first citywide zoning ordinance in this country was passed in New York in 1916. It would not have been adopted without the support of realtors and businessmen who regarded it as a "modest proposal," merely a needed prop for the real estate industry. Reformers and homeowner organizations made huge concessions to obtain their suport, but these did not last long. The "prop" soon began to take over. The original New York ordinance had only three districts: residence, business, and unrestricted. At last count that ordinance contained sixty-six districts plus innumerable other complexities. Any relation between New York's current ordinance and the original one is largely coincidental.

The constantly expanding zoning process reflects the fact that land use regulation can never successfully fulfill the varied intentions and expectations of the public. Satisfying the interests of some alienates others or creates new problems. No matter how perfect the plan, it will still have to favor certain groups over others. As pendulums swing and preferences and political powers change, losers will become winners, and cause the law to be altered in their behalf. A similar scenario applies to state and federal land use controls.

It is also the story of many other programs. Once a toehold has been established by passage of regulatory legislation, there is no predicting the future course, only that the controls are likely to inflate vastly over the years. Nothing prevents successive Congresses from amending into oblivion carefully prepared deals that made possible the adoption of the original legislation.

Nor, because of the uncertainties of the legislative process, can anyone be sure that a bill will become law until it has been voted in and not vetoed. In May 1973 I conversed with over a dozen people in Washington—congressmen and others who were active opponents or proponents of federal land use regulation. Without exception, they assured me that some such act would pass in that Congress. They were wrong; the legislation was defeated in 1974. The measure was back again in Congress in 1975 and was not even able to obtain approval in committee. A determined fight by opponents kept the House bill from passing. Had they surrendered or compromised, it is possible Congress might by now be considering amendments.

The outlook for passage of such legislation at state levels has also dimmed. Although it still looms large, almost daily the environmentalist tide seems to recede. It has sustained significant losses recently in the courts, in legislatures, and in local elections. Perhaps indicative of a new mood, the voters of Santa Barbara County, California, where the large oil spill occurred, elected in early 1975 to allow an oil refinery to be built over the vociferous objections of the environmentalists.

Regulation is not necessarily the wave of the future. It may well be, however, if its logical opponents desert the cause. Regulation has been getting a bad press. Favoring regulation is no longer an automatic road to popularity and opposing environmental schemes has become increasingly respectable, even in the liberal press. Realtors who become highly enthusiastic about urban planning are liable to earn chuckles and not admiration. The times may be more appropriate for repealing than enacting laws.

More than land use regulation is at issue. Such legislation will create powerful new layers of government and diminish further the private enterprise system. The people's right to own and use property will be severely weakened, perhaps in time effectively destroyed. No believer in a free society can be complacent about those prospects.

Ideas and beliefs ought not to be traded like goods on a counter. Moreover, opportunism destroys credibility. Who is going to believe the businessmen's commitment to private enterprise when they support measures to immobilize it? We would normally expect that people who use and benefit from a system of private property would vigorously uphold it. Regrettably, businessmen have not always responded to that calling. The slide to collectivism is in part due to their failure. They must stand up—and opposition to further government control of the land is the least that can be asked of them.

The Taking Clause

The Public Interest, Property Rights, and Taking

There is a small clause in the Constitution of the United States that does not frequently claim public attention; yet, its importance cannot be overestimated. It is part of the Bill of Rights contained in the Constitution and it is the one that protects the individual against government greed. I refer to that last clause of the Fifth Amendment to the Constitution, which reads ". . . nor shall private property be taken for public use without just compensation." This is known as the "taking clause," for it prevents the government from taking away or confiscating the property rights of the individual.

There would seem to be nothing extraordinary about a rule in a nontotalitarian society that requires government to pay for property it takes or acquires from its constituents. It places the government in the same status as any stranger to the property—and, after all, government consists of a great many strangers. It is a prohibition against theft by government in a sense comparable to innumerable other laws that prohibit theft by any of its citizens.

Under the terms of this clause, the courts have upheld as legal many laws that deprive owners of valuable property interests. Still, over the years, even as there has been this erosion of property rights, the clause has tended at least to prevent outright confiscation of property and many zoning and other regulatory laws have been invalidated.

It costs more money to buy property than to take it—and this obvious fact has been a cause of concern to those who believe that government can use the property more wisely than its owner. The Rockefeller Task Force on Land Use and Urban Growth has expressed concern that the taking clause will make excessively expensive the land use policies that they would like adopted and that they consider to be in the public interest. [8] They propose that more land be restricted for open space and for other purposes they believe desirable, and they find the taking clause to be a serious obstacle to these objectives. The Task Force, therefore, has suggested that the whole taking issue be reconsidered and that henceforth government should be able to control the use of land with minimum restraint from the courts: "It is important that state and local legislative bodies adopt stringent planning and regulatory legislation whenever they feel it fair and necessary to achieve land use objectives." [9]

Comparable arguments can be made with respect to any scarce resource of commodity—and we may expect other "task forces" to proceed on other fronts. There are always some benefits to be derived by taking from some and giving to others. Two members of the Task Force are high officials of major banks, and surely would agree that regulations lowering the bank rate from 10 percent to 2 percent would benefit many. But such regulations would also destroy our banking system, which benefits the vast majority.

The inevitable results of increasing the number and amount of such controls is to impair the freedom of the individual to acquire and own property—in all likelihood a freedom considered a prime one by most people.

Nor is it fair that the burden for providing the presumed welfare of others should be borne by the owners of only those properties "stringently regulated" for public purposes. The accident of ownership and location would select those persons in society to carry the burden of paying for benefits that will accrue to others. It amounts to a rather crude way of redistributing wealth on a most unfair and irrational basis.

The taking clause not only serves the equitable and moral concerns set forth here, but it also furthers very functional values in our society. First, when things cost nothing, there is no limitation upon their acquisition. This being a time when many municipalities and individuals would like to curb further growth, they could do so if there were no cost involved in restricting much of the balance of their land for open space or very low density development. A great amount of land would thereby be removed overall from development or production to the detriment of business, employment, industry, agriculture, housing, etc.

America, as a land of parks and open space, would also be America, the land of worse housing and higher rents. Budgetary considerations at least curb an insatiable government appetite and operate to create a more appropriate and equitable allocation of our resources.

Second, the incentives of our society for owners and developers to own and use land for productive purposes would be destroyed. Why own land or contemplate using it if government at its whim can preempt it for other purposes? Or if one does own land zoned for certain purposes, one would rush to use it before the politicians changed their minds. At the very least, a more chaotic market would result.

The Bill of Rights has often thwarted the aims and desires of government and its officials, and that is exactly the effect the authors intended: to protect the individual against the might of government.

True to form, the taking clause worries officials of the Council on Environmental Quality, the federal environmental agency that has been considering land use legislation. In what appears to be an effort to minimize the legal importance of this clause, the council has published and distributed a 329 page book entitled *The Taking Issue*.[10] The book fails to mention that major victims, in addition to those who own certain properties, would be those who benefit from a system allowing private ownership—and that, in the final analysis, includes just about everyone.

Zoning and International Law

Nothing seems more removed from international law than local zoning. Yet, there is an interesting relationship. Zoning restricts the use of private property, sometimes to a degree that virtually expropriates it. If that action were directed against American owned land or property in a foreign country, the U.S. State Department would denounce it as contrary to international law and call for payment of just compensation.

There is a difference to be sure. Foreign expropriation measures are often directed at specific nationals, which is not the case in zoning. Land use regulations intended only for, say, English or French companies would fail constitutionally as discriminatory.

The similarity is that the laws in both instances are being adopted supposedly in the public interest. The foreign law makers usually say that expropriation decrees are designed to promote the overall good, not simply harm the owners. That is another version of the argument used to justify arbitrary zoning.

An interesting double standard exists. An American firm that owns land in a foreign nation would have the support of the United States government against efforts by that country to take it away. It is far less likely that many agencies of our government would take a comparable stand in a domestic matter. Government officials are not alone, of course, in making this distinction. Some prominent people that one would expect not to be happy about foreign takings seem enthusiastic about the domestic variety. An example is the Rockefeller Task Force:

It is time that the U.S. Supreme Court re-examine its earlier precedents that seem to require a balancing of public benefit against land value loss in every case and declare that when the protection of natural, cultural or aesthetic resources or the assurance of orderly development are involved, a mere loss in land value will never be justification for invalidating the regulation of land use.[11]

If there is any basis whatever for the taking clause, it must be to stop government from eliminating property values on the basis of such highly subjective and vague terms as, "natural," "cultural," "aesthetic," or "orderly development." Every right in the Constitution would be meaningless if legislatures had unlimited power to determine the public interest. No government in history, regardless of the horrors it perpetrated, has ever acknowledged that it acted for the "public bad."

The views of the Rockefeller Task Force could be used by foreign countries to justify confiscation of American owned property. The United States position on taking by other nations is much to the contrary, however, and was set forth by Secretary of State Hull in a letter to the Mexican Ambassador in July 1938. Beginning in 1915 Mexico had taken numerous moderate-size farms owned by Americans without compensating the owners. The Mexicans contended that their actions were necessary to carry out a program essential to social betterment. Secretary Hull protested:

The issue is not whether Mexico should pursue social and economic policies designed to improve the standards of living of its people. The issue is whether in pursuing them the property of American nationals may be taken by the Mexican government without making prompt payment of just compensation to the owner in accordance with the universally recognized rules of law and equity.

If the rule of law were otherwise, governments would be free to take property far beyond their ability and willingness to pay and the owners would be without recourse.[12]

Hull's interpretations are similar to rules appearing in the most recent *Restatement, Foreign Relations Law of the United States,*[13] written by leading authorities in the field. Although the United Nations and many countries do not accept this position, most Western nations adhere to it. The Rockefeller report notwithstanding, it is difficult to conceive of an orderly society or world in the absence of such a standard.

Notes

1. Coase, *Economists and Public Policy,* in LARGE CORPORATIONS IN A CHANGING SOCIETY 169 (J. Weston, ed. 1974). Strong criticism of the operations of the regulatory process have come also from writers who favor greater government involvement in economic activity. Reich, *The Law of the Planned Society,* 75 YALE L.J. 799 (1966); Popper, *Land Use Reform–Illusion or Reality?,* PLANNING 14 (ASPO Sept. 1974). *See generally* LOWI, THE END OF LIBERALISM (1969) and THE POLITICS OF DISORDER (1971).

2. Interesting insights into federal regulation are given by two former commissioners of the Federal Trade Commission. Elman, *Administrative Reform of the Federal Trade Commission,* 59 GEO. L.J. 777 (1971); L. MASON, THE LANGUAGE OF DISSENT (Cleveland: World Publishing Co. 1959).

3. DERTHICK, NEW TOWNS IN-TOWN (Washington, D.C.: The Urban Institute, 1972).

4. H.R. 3510, the land use bill introduced in the House in 1975, uses the term "areas of critical state concern" to incorporate most of the objectives of the quoted portions of H.R. 10294. I have quoted the more extensive language of the earlier bill because it is probably more indicative of the goals of the sponsors and supporting organiza-

tion. One major difference is the elimination of "significant agricultural and grazing land" in H.R. 3510 as areas of critical state concern. This was done to reduce opposition of farmers' organizations, but apparently without success. H.R. 3510 would still require state regulatory authority over land used for agriculture.

5. CALIFORNIA COASTAL ZONE CONSERVATION COMMISSION, ANNUAL REPORT (1973).

6. M. Bruce Johnson, *Piracy on the California Coast*, REASON, July 1974.

7. TASK FORCE REPORT Sponsored by Rockefeller Brothers Fund, THE USE OF LAND: A CITIZEN'S POLICY GUIDE TO URBAN GROWTH, Chap. I (N.Y: Crowell Co. 1973).

8. *Ibid.*

9. *Ibid.* at 173.

10. BOSSELMAN, CALLIES & BANTA, THE TAKING ISSUE (U.S. Gov't Printing Office 1973).

11. ROCKEFELLER TASK FORCE REPORT at 175.

12. 3 HACKWORTH, INTERNATIONAL LAW 655-665 (1942).

13. RESTATEMENT (2nd) FOREIGN RELATIONS LAW OF THE UNITED STATES, 553-571 (1965).

5

The Ever-Changing Judicial Climate

Petaluma

Cities attain prominence for a variety of reasons. One is that they become involved in what lawyers term "landmark" litigation. This is the explanation for the fame achieved in the 1970s by Petaluma, California. It made the national headlines when a federal court judge ruled its growth control policies were unconstitutional,[1] and again when a three judge panel of the U.S. Ninth Circuit Court of Appeals unanimously reversed that decision.[2] Another spate of stories and editorials can be anticipated if or when the U.S. Supreme Court rules on the case.

Petaluma is located about 45 miles North of San Francisco and is considered part of the San Francisco Bay area metropolitan region. Until the recent litigation, it had been known primarily for dairy and poultry production. It grew from about 10,000 in 1950 to over 30,000 in 1972. The city council in 1971 adopted a development policy to control growth and maintain what was left of its "small town character and surrounding open space."

Projections made on the basis of its growth rate had indicated that by 1985, the city's population would be 77,000. In an effort to reduce that number to 55,000, the city adopted a series of regulations, one of which imposed a maximum ceiling of 2500 developmental dwelling units for the five year period 1973 to 77. Building permits were to be allotted at the rate of approximately 500 per year during that period. Exempt from this limitation were permits for all projects of four units or less. Because of this exemption, it is difficult to determine the precise impact of the permit controls. Two thousand housing permits were issued in the two year period of 1970 to 1971. The trial court found that the plan would prevent the construction of about one-half to two-thirds of the market demand for housing units. It also concluded that although the plan was ostensibly limited to a five year period, official attempts were made to perpetuate it beyond 1977. The circuit court was less certain as to the effect, and assumed for purposes of its decision, that the 500 development unit growth rate "is in fact below the reasonably anticipated market demand for such units and that absent the Petaluma Plan, the City would grow at a faster rate."

Petaluma's is the ultimate zoning ordinance. The city made an effort to control residential development minutely and few zoning ordinances have gone as far. Many suburbs have, through their zoning ordinances, sought indirectly to achieve similar results by low density and open space requirements and strict limitations on apartment construction. Through the device of the planned unit development, they have also been able to determine the kind of units that are built, and the amount of open space and recreational facilities that will be required within the complex.

Petaluma's plan was indeed detailed. Among other things, it provided for a specified allocation of building permits for east and west portions of the city and between single and multi-family dwellings, a 200 foot green belt extending around the city, the establishment of an eight to twelve percent quota for housing for low and moderate income persons, and policies for determining how building permit applications would be approved.

Federal District Judge Burke ruled that Petaluma's regulations violated the constitutional right to travel. While the Constitution contains no provision explicitly mentioning this right, the U.S. Supreme Court, in a long line of cases beginning in 1867, has protected the freedom of citizens to travel unimpeded from one state to another.[3]

The Supreme Court has gradually been extending this right to include migration and settlement, and has declared unconstitutional a number of laws that did not accord recent migrants to a state or county the same rights as those given existing residents. Judge Burke decided that Petaluma's ordinances, by limiting the number of people who could live in the city had interfered with the right of citizens to migrate and settle in places of their own choosing.

This issue was argued in a 1974 U.S. Supreme Court case concerning the Village of Belle Terre, New York, which had adopted an ordinance prohibiting more than two unmarried and unrelated adults from living together in one house. The Court said that since the ordinance was not aimed at transients, there was no infringement of the right to travel.[4]

Burke said the Belle Terre case was not relevant to the Petaluma situation. His opinion relies in large measure on decisions of the Pennsylvania Supreme Court which have declared unconstitutional, ordinances that establish certain minimum lot sizes or do not provide for apartment zoning.[5] The Pennsylvania court has ruled such restrictions as deliberately exclusionary and therefore unconstitutional. It did not refer to the right to travel, but Judge Burke concluded that the underlying rationale of those cases is consistent with this right.

The circuit court made no decision on the right to travel. It held that this issue could not be raised in this case since none of those suing were seeking housing in Petaluma. For this point, the court relied on a U.S. Supreme Court opinion concerning Penfield, New York, issued in June 1975, which appears to limit suits by nonresidents to those persons seeking to live in a particular housing development.[6]

Once it had disposed of the right to travel issue, the court treated the case as it would a typical zoning controversy. The question in such cases is whether there is a reasonable basis for the regulation, that is, whether the municipality is justified in denying an owner of property the opportunity to use it as he or she desires. Courts have been going through such a reasoning process even since the U.S. Supreme Court decided in 1926 in the Euclid (Ohio) case that zoning was constitutional.[7]

The standard of reasonableness is a very broad one and tends to favor the municipality, especially since the courts presume that the regulation in question is valid. The burden is on those who contest it to prove otherwise.

The Court of Appeals decided that it was reasonable for a city to adopt laws to preserve its small town character, its open spaces and low density of population, and to grow at an orderly and deliberate pace. The court likened the case to two others in which zoning ordinances have been upheld. One of these was the Belle Terre decision, and the other was a case involving the Town of Los Altos Hills, California, in which the same circuit court upheld a minimum lot size requirement of one acre.[8]

Neither case appears to support the Petaluma decision. The Village of Belle Terre consists of about 220 residences with a population of 700. That case involved a constitutional challenge premised on rights of unrelated tenants to live together in a single family residence contrary to the zoning ordinance. While it is correct, as

the circuit court said, that the zoning ordinance of the village prevented conversion of any residence to multifamily housing and
thereby prevented future growth, the case presented only the question of multiple occupancy by the tenants.

Moreover, it is difficult to compare a very small built-up community without vacant land to a vastly greater one with considerable
amounts of vacant land and subject to strong housing pressures. The
Belle Terre case might take on some comparability if a 50 or 100 unit
apartment building had been proposed, not merely the invalidation
of zoning for the sake of communal living.

In the Los Altos Hills case, the one acre minimum was likewise
relatively minor, compared to the much more onerous restrictions of
Petaluma. It surely does not follow that if one acre zoning is valid,
five, twenty, or forty acre zoning will likewise be legal. Petaluma's
restrictions are much more comparable to a twenty, rather than a
one acre, limitation. The courts in zoning matters have continually
said that each case stands on its own facts. While a fifteen acre
minimum lot size may be a reasonable requirement in a rural area, it
would surely not be legal in downtown San Francisco.

The circuit court judges acknowledged that laws designed to
further the interests of a municipality may be harmful to those living
in the area or region in which it is located. Judge Burke's opinion had
shown in great detail the adverse effects of the Petaluma plan on
housing conditions elsewhere in the San Francisco metropolitan
area. The circuit judges reply was that these were problems for
legislatures and not courts:

If the present system of delegated zoning power does not effectively serve
the state interest, in furthering the general welfare of the region or entire
state, it is the state legislature's and not the federal court's role to intervene
and adjust the system. . . . [T]he federal court is not a super zoning board
and should not be called upon to mark the point upon which legitimate local
interests in promoting the welfare of the community are outweighed by
legitimate regional interests.

On this basis, it is hard to envision any set of zoning rules that this
court would remove. Yet, many, possibly most, state courts would
have thrown out the Petaluma type restrictions. Pennsylvania[9] and
Virginia[10] courts, for example, have taken a dim view of much less
restrictive rules. When the U.S. Supreme Court validated zoning, it
certainly did not say that a municipality could do anything it wanted

in the name of zoning. That court has only considered five zoning ordinances in about fifty years, and has overruled two. In 1929, it nullified a zoning ordinance in Cambridge, Mass., which it held unreasonably restricted a landowner's right to use his property.[11] The same court also invalidated a zoning ordinance of Seattle, Washington.[12]

The *Euclid* decision, in erecting the reasonableness test did not bar courts from considering regional impact in deciding whether that test had been met. There is language in the case that would indicate just the reverse. One of the most noted sentences of that opinion is the following:

It is not meant by this, however, to exclude the possibility of cases where the general public interest would so far outweigh the interest of the municipality that the municipality would not be allowed to stand in the way.[13]

This statement seems directly contrary to the position taken by the circuit court. Numerous zoning decisions have taken into account matters outside of the municipality.

Regional considerations need not have been considered, however, for the circuit court to have found that Petaluma imposed unreasonable and improper restraints on the use of land within the city. Consider what occurs to land values upon the adoption of the Petaluma plan. In the usual situation, value of land is largely dependent on zoning and its availability and desirability for building purposes. Those parcels most in demand will have a relatively high value. Petaluma's quota system changes all of that, except for the smaller sites that could be developed with one to four units. Builders would not want to pay more for any tract than its value for one to four units, unless they knew the land could be used for the erection of more units, and they would not know this until the annual selection process takes place.

This means that until the tract is earmarked for building under the quota, those who must sell, may have to do so at a very low price. Two adjoining similar properties, each consisting of, say ten acres, would have vastly different values if only one of them chanced to be included in the building quota for that year. Although thousands of acres would be left in legal limbo and values kept at a minimum, the landowners would still have to continue making tax payments.

Such serious deprivations of property values undermine the

validity of the city's regulations. The taking clause of the Fifth Amendment provides that private property shall not be taken for public use without just compensation. While there is loss of value frequently under zoning, the degree to which this occurs is a consideration in applying the reasonableness test. Allowing such substantial losses in values as will occur in Petaluma would make meaningless constitutional protections against confiscation of property.

There is little reference in the Petaluma decision to the rights of property owners. This is understandable since plaintiffs premised their arguments largely on the right to travel and sociological impact. Interestingly enough, the same circuit court earlier in the year in a case brought by Union Oil Company and others, against the Secretary of the Interior, displayed concern that the Secretary's regulations violated the taking clause. It stated that regulation of private property can become so onerous as to constitute a taking of it, and sent that case back for further findings on this issue to the lower court which had dismissed the suit.[14]

Nor did the court consider adequately the consequences of a quota system. A quota means that some persons who would otherwise have the opportunity to use and develop their property will be denied it. The Petaluma authorities will have to make these selections, and they will have to use standards that must necessarily be subjective and often arbitrary. Enormous differences of opinion can exist on what are the most pleasing structures, the excellence of design and environmental suitability, some of the criteria under the city's plan.

There will be considerable opportunities for graft, moral corruption and political abuse. One likely result is that the city will require houses to have extras and frills consumers do not desire, nor with to pay for—in effect an admission price into the city. Another consequence is that the competitive system under which our economy is supposed to operate will be effectively barred from Petaluma. The decisions on buildings will be made there primarily by local politicians and officials, and not by businessmen and consumers. Were this practice to spread across the country it would further compromise our private enterprise system.

Turning to regional consequences, there are three possibilities as to what will result from Petaluma's exclusionary policies. First, more housing will be built in other nearby communities. Second, housing will be built in areas not presently used for urban purposes. Third, some of the demand for housing will remain unsatisfied.

It is likely that other cities will either retaliate or find the Petaluma Plan attractive and if they adopt similar policies, the total number excluded from existing communities in the area will increase. This means that either less housing will be build or the excluded housing will be located in rural areas. Probably a certain amount of both will occur. The rural areas are not likely to yield nearly as much housing. Demand is less there and these areas have fewer utilities and facilities to accomodate construction.

This will be harmful to housing needs. More housing is obviously needed. Housing starts were off substantially in 1974 and 75. Billions of dollars are being spent by the federal government to create better housing conditions. It would be absurd that the nation's goals of stimulating more and better housing should be frustrated by local goals of limiting housing. It is equally inexcusable that federal policies to encourage business and development and competition should be impeded by local policies that operate to discourage them.

Serious problems will also be created if exclusionary housing policies cause more rural and farm land to be urbanized. A recent report prepared for government agencies pointed with alarm to the increased urbanization of rural lands.[15] The report indicated that 2,000 acres per day were changing from rural to urban property. Petaluma-type policies will considerably augment that amount, at a time when a maximum amount of land should be available for farming, grazing and mining. Thousands of acres will be wasted for unnecessary urban development.

If the annual demand is for 1,000 to 1,500 permits as Judge Burke assumed, and only 500 are issued, the supply will be much less than the demand and the price of new housing will significantly appreciate. The wealthiest one-third and one-half of the families who want to settle there will best be able to do so. Should other new communities follow suit, the economic discrepancies between older and newer areas will widen substantially. The exclusionary communities will become richer as the others become poorer. Since wealthier people can better afford to pay property taxes and live in more luxurious accomodations, it would be almost foolhardy for a locality not to pursue the Petaluma plan. Thereby, these communities will shift the urban burdens of the nation to the bigger cities where poorer portions of the population will remain locked in.

These adversities caused by Petaluma's plan will not be alleviated by its sub-quota for low and moderate income families. Eight to twelve percent of Petaluma's quota must be for this group, which roughly approximates 50 units of the 500. A provision of 50 units of one kind of housing can hardly justify the exclusion of possibly 500 units of another. Nor is it fair to give special preferential treatment to a few fortunate members of one class.

The 500 excluded units would be occupied by wealthier people, but the construction of them would more than compensate poorer people for the loss of 50 new units. The University of Michigan's filtering study[16] found that the building and occupancy of a new housing unit results in an additional housing opportunity for low and moderate income families. While it is conceivable that all the units excluded by Petaluma might be built elsewhere, it is most unlikely that this would occur, as previously suggested.

Implicit in the creation of such a subquota is the assumption that it will provide decent housing to a group that presently cannot obtain it. The limitations in building established by the overall quota, however, are likely to result in adverse housing conditions for many persons with incomes greater than those in the moderate and low income categories. Nor does the establishment of such a subquota necessarily mean it will or can be satisfied. Low and moderate income housing requires public subsidies which are not that readily available. Ironically, funds to build it will come from taxpayers excluded from Petaluma. (The serious limitations of subsidized housing are discussed in various other portions of this book).

According to undisputed expert testimony at the trial of the case, duly reported in the circuit court's opinion, if the Petaluma plan were to be adopted by municipalities throughout the region, the shortfall in needed housing in the region for the decade 1970 to 1980 would be 105,000 units, or 25 percent of the units it was said are needed. It was further testified that there would be a resultant decline in regional housing stock quality, a loss of housing mobility and a deterioration especially in the housing available to those with real incomes of $14,000 per year or less.

Petaluma-type barriers appear contrary to the nature of the union as one country. Localities should not feather their own nexts at the expense of all others. Los Angeles, Chicago and New York might still be rural enclaves if their original settlers had the power to keep them that way. The first thousand or million could have prevented millions of followers from locating there. Immensely greater portions of land would have been urbanized. Great artificial restraints would have been placed on mobility and movement in this country. There would have been less housing and it would have cost more.

Activism and Restraint

A major attack against zoning emanates from certain civil rights-social activist organizations. They do not seek to abolish zoning, but want it changed sufficiently to enable low- and moderate-income housing to be built in the affluent suburbs. In addition to seeking relief through political action, they have turned to the courts, contending that prevailing zoning practices are unconstitutional because they exclude housing for poorer people.

These groups were victorious early in 1975 in New Jersey. The Supreme Court of the state ruled that developing suburbs must provide in their zoning ordinances for housing to be occupied by the less affluent.[17] Those who sue in such cases often do not live in the localities whose ordinances they are challenging. The suits allege that certain low-income persons, often members of minority groups, want to live in the suburb but cannot because of "exclusionary" zoning. These suits are directed against general practices, and do not usually concern a specific development.

This form of attack suffered a serious defeat when a sharply divided U.S. Supreme Court in a suit against the town of Penfield, N.Y. (a suburb of Rochester), ruled by a five to four margin that non-residents are not entitled to sue for this relief; legally speaking, that they lacked "standing" to sue.[18] The majority opinion is contrary to the position of the New Jersey high court which allows standing in such cases for non-residents.

The Penfield case was decided solely on the standing issue and did not go into the merits of the town's zoning ordinance. Not everyone with a grievance is entitled under the Constitution to file for redress in the federal courts, and the question of who can sue is not always clear. One of the prerequisites is "standing," often, as in this case, a highly debatable standard. The rule established by the Penfield opinion is that standing will be allowed those who can demonstrate that zoning practices harm them personally and "would benefit in a tangible way from the court's intervention." This comes close to limiting federal court relief only to those who can show they are harmed by a locality's rejection of a particular housing project.

Most commentators will probably attribute the Penfield decision to the court majority's inclination to judicial restraint. The opinion may also reflect a desire of these judges not to tamper with local zoning. Given the apparent situation in Penfield, however, it is quite likely that the Court over which former Chief Justice Earl Warren presided would have to come to a different decision, one more consistent with the New Jersey rule. The Warren Court was activist, prone to create a judicial remedy when it found what it regarded as a social wrong. Its supporters want the judiciary to resolve critical problems that legislatures and executives fail to act on, although at times this might necessitate some law making.

The advocates of judicial restraint, on the other hand, contend that the role of the courts should be strictly limited. They reject the notion that judges should establish new laws. Time has shown that these arguments are also well-founded in pragmatism. Judicial activism appears to work no better than the legislative variety, often doing more harm than good. Consider, for example, the consequences of a judicial decision that suburbs like Penfield must zone for lesser income housing. Were such a ruling to be made, legal attacks on the basis of that single issue would be instituted against suburbs across the country. The benefits would not be worth the turmoil, however.

Low- and moderate-income housing developments require subsidies and the judiciary, for all of its wisdom, has not yet discovered ways to create money. Congress has to appropriate it, and, for the foreseeable future at least, could not possibly provide enough to erect such projects for more than a small fraction of the nation's suburbs. The suburbs that were forced (or willing) to accept projects would in all probability get off the judicial hook for all of their other zoning indiscretions. There would then be little to prevent them from elevating building and zoning requirements and thereby causing overall less housing to be produced. That drama is already playing suburbia, and the courts surely should not make it compulsory.

Housing subsidies are borne by all taxpayers, including, of course, the poorer ones who do not move into those projects. Government borrowing to provide them would add to the demand for money, increasing pressures on interest rates. Experience has also shown that these projects are much more costly and far less successful than privately financed construction.

New Jersey: A Study in Change

Balanced Communities

When pendulums swing, sometimes they swing with a vengeance. One example is provided by the state of New Jersey, once a stronghold of highly restrictive zoning, where courts have been busily erasing zoning regulations.

In the 1970s a judicial storm developed to compensate for the many decades when the courts there almost invariably upheld the zoning policies of local governments. As a result of these policies, there is a serious imbalance in housing opportunities in that state, to the detriment of those of average and less income levels. It may be a lesson to those communities presently concocting new and stricter zoning laws designed to limit development of the land.

By 1973 at least seven cases in trial and intermediate courts had overturned all or parts of zoning ordinances because they prevented construction of apartments or homes for families of about average or below average incomes. The Supreme Court of the state has responded favorably to the new approach.[19]

Perhaps the most dramatic decision occurred in Bergen County in October 1973, when a trial court judge ruled that the courts have power to rezone municipalities and declared that he would rezone a town to provide for multifamily housing.[20] The judge's action was prompted by the failure of that town's governing council and planning board to follow his order to zone land for apartments that he had entered in a lawsuit involving a proposed $7 million, 520-unit garden apartment development. A judge in another county was quoted as saying that as a result of some of the decisions in these cases, the current state planning act was not really the law in New Jersey any longer.[21]

The municipalities have defended their zoning on the basis that existing schools and sewer and water facilities were inadequate to serve an expanded population, and that substantial public expenditures would be required to provide them. They have also raised the usual antigrowth arguments: increased traffic and congestion and the alleged undesirability of high-density development. In rejecting these arguments, the courts have in effect found that the legal interests of those who want the opportunity to move into the community outweigh the interests of those fortunate enough to have gotten there first.

It is regretable that these practices have forced the judiciary to take such a prominent role in land use. While these courts seemingly are carrying out the traditional role of the judiciary to uphold minority rights—in these cases, those relating to mobility and housing opportunities—a less coercive solution is much to be preferred.

Judges are no better qualified to determine "proper" land use than are the municipalities. Both the legislative and judicial branches should instead be seeking solutions consistent with freedom and not coercion, which means in short, restoring freedom to the marketplace that will allow more producers to build and more consumers to buy housing.

These decisions have caused planners, many of whom share responsibility for these problems, to begin thinking in terms of zoning for balanced communities, which is to say, here we go again with another grandiose zoning scheme destined to meet the usual fate of its predecessors. It can be expected that planners will begin defining the elements of balanced communities, which will be anything but balanced.

How can anyone, after all, establish the proper amount of housing for low, middle, and upper income families, for ethnic and racial minorities, and for the many categories within these categories? How do you force builders to comply with the quotas? Regardless of the merits of the schemes, moreover, political pressures are likely to emasculate them. The zoning plan and zoning product are rarely the same thing.

There are communities that come close to being balanced, and those are the ones that have not erected legal barriers excluding certain groups on the basis of planners' speculations and political expediencies. These are the communities that have been wise enough not to adopt zoning. In the absence of zoning, builders and developers will provide housing in accordance with what people want and can are are willing to pay for, and just the increase in supply alone will benefit every housing consumer from the richest to the poorest.

There is, consequently, only one major city in this country where housing is reasonably balanced, and that is the city without zoning—Houston, Texas. And that city is balanced precisely because no person or group has tried to balance it.

Affirmative Zoning

The New Jersey Supreme Court has come down hard on suburban zoning. In a long awaited decision involving the township of Mount Laurel, the court told suburbs that they had to provide zoning to accommodate housing for low- and moderate-income families.[22]

Justice Frederick Hall wrote the opinion and that fact reveals the change in zoning climate that has occurred in the state. Thirteen years ago Hall was one of the dissenters in a five to two decision that upheld the authority of a locality to exclude mobile home parks completely from its borders. He then sharply criticized the use of the zoning power to keep out the kind of housing existing residents deemed undesirable.[23]

Time has vindicated Hall's dissenting opinion and the court has come full circle. As a result of the Mount Laurel case, suburbs in that state may no longer reject housing for poorer people. Indeed, they must provide for it in their zoning laws. The makeup of the supreme court had changed, but perhaps more importantly, so had the general awareness of the operation of zoning. Because the New Jersey courts had in the past done little to restrain them, municipalities had become highly restrictive, doing about what they wanted in zoning matters.

In a concurring opinion in the Mount Laurel case, Justice Pashman detailed the regulatory devices by which exclusion has been accomplished. He categorized them into six groups: minimum house size requirements, minimum lot size and frontage requirements, prohibition of multifamily housing, restrictions on a number of bedrooms in apartments to limit school children, prohibition of mobile homes, and overzoning for nonresidential uses.

He favored a stronger policy than the other judges, going beyond the provision of sufficient zoning and advocating that all localities, not just suburbs, be required to provide a fair share of housing needs. Said Pashman: "Exclusionary zoning is a problem of such magnitude and depth as to require that the court extend these principles to all municipalities . . . and that the court establish a policy of active judicial enforcement. . . ."

Were Pashman's views to prevail in time as Hall's have, the court in effect would become a supreme zoning and housing board, with the strong possibility of creating complications and turmoil comparable to what is presently occurring in court directed school busing. Municipalities consequently might face even more drastic action in the future.

Unlike their brethren in many other states, the judges in New Jersey are obviously well aware of the abuses prevalent under zoning and can be expected to monitor it. There is no reason, however, to conclude that they will be better zoners than the politicians.

Thus, the serious concern the court has shown for more balanced housing will probably lead to overzoning for low- and moderate-income housing. Most such housing requires government subsidies and there is relatively little available. Nor does zoning for certain kinds of housing automatically result in such housing.

Regardless of how moderate the zoning is the land will still remain vacant if it is not economically feasible for a builder to purchase and develop it. When land is zoned for uses not in demand, less will be available for what is wanted and lot prices will rise accordingly. Exclusion of those not able to afford the increased cost will result.

It is highly questionable that only zoning has been holding back minorities and people of lesser means and that they will now flock to the suburbs. Land costs are high, public transportation is limited, and living is more expensive and frequently less comfortable in suburbia for poorer people. Undoubtedly many were barred in the past and should be allowed every opportunity to locate there. The only institution that can reasonably make this evaluation, however, is the marketplace, which operates on a very pragmatic and nontheoretical level

In essence, the New Jersey court has concluded that once government controls are invoked, they must not be used by any group or groups against all others. The problem is that only the courts can set standards by which to determine if this has happened. When the suburbs do not become balanced as some would like, lawsuits are bound to follow, causing greater judicial intervention in local matters, sometimes to the good and probably at least as often for the worst.

In New Jersey suburban zoning, home owner supremacy appears to have ended and judicial dominance begun. Suburbanites might well consider whether the elimination of zoning is not preferable to the continual threat of the judiciary.

Private Rights and Public Interest

Suppose that some city or county took away from certain families of average income hundreds or thousands of dollars and distributed the money to the poor and ailing, or used it to acquire a park or site for a school, or to remove pollution from the air and water. In spite of these humanitarian and charitable motives, most anyone who believed in a just and orderly society would strongly condemn such arbitrary action. For ours is supposed to and should be a society that protects the rights of the individual. That is what distinguishes it from a totalitarian one where the individual is submerged to the might of the state, whether it be for good or for evil. The simplest notions of justice would seem to require that the cost of paying for society's burdens be spread over the population on the basis of some rational system of taxation.

Ronald and Kathryn Just of Porterfield, Wisconsin are among those who have learned that these concepts are not always operative in this country. Their case has achieved considerable notoriety but not because they were deprived of valuable rights. On the contrary, the case is being heralded in environmental circles because it gives enormous powers to government to control the use of land.

Hardly a murmur has come from those many organizations across the country ostensibly dedicated to protecting individual rights—this apparently because property rights are involved, and there has been a great tendency to ignore the enormous harm that can result to people when they are deprived of their property.

In April of 1961 the Justs purchased thirty-six acres of land in Marinette County, Wisconsin, of which 1,266 feet fronted on Lake Noquebay. They planned to sell most of it and build a house for themselves on the balance. By 1967 they had made five sales, leaving them a tract fronting about 367 feet on the lake. They wanted to sell another portion and build a house on the remainder.

The Justs are wage earners of modest means. Ronald Just is employed as a machine driver-operator, and Kathryn, a bookkeeper-secretary. In 1967 they were in their late thirties.

In the last half of 1967, pursuant to authority given by a law of the state concerning water pollution, Marinette County adopted an ordinance controlling the use of privately owned shorelands, which forbid the Justs from using their land to construct any residential buildings. A limited number of uses were allowed but none had more than very minor, if any, commercial value. The ordinance also prohibited the Justs from placing specified amounts of fill on the land without obtaining a conditional use permit from the county. If they violated this ordinance, they were subject to a civil forfeiture of $10 to $200 per day. In February and March of 1968 Mr. Just, without securing a conditional use permit, placed more fill on the land than was permitted.

So began a long and costly legal struggle terminating with an opinion by the supreme court of that state in October 1972, holding that the ordinance was constitutional and the Justs had violated it.[24] The basis of that opinion was that the public interest in stopping the "despoliation of natural resources" was greater than the owner's right to use his property. What the court failed to perceive was that in our society there is no greater public interest than the right of the individual to be secure against the state. The oft-quoted observation of Justice Oliver Wendell Holmes is clearly on point: "We are in danger of forgetting that a strong public desire to improve the public condition is not enough to warrant achieving the desire by a shorter cut than the constitutional way of paying for the change."[25]

The court contended that the Justs property was not being confiscated since some uses were still allowed. The Justs can no longer use their property for building, nor is it feasible for farming. They will be forced to buy land elsewhere for their house. Effectively, the Justs have been deprived of thousands of dollars, possibly as much as $15,000—a great sum for people in their circumstances. They have also sustained cost in money, time, and energy involved in fighting city hall, as they have explained:

We could write a book about what transpired before we finally got into the Wisconsin Supreme Court. From the lowly county court way up to the top, we have seen courtrooms turned into something that would resemble political arenas. We lived through five years of offers of "deals" by petty politicians, political officials losing papers that were vital to our case, delay upon delay for the most feeble of excuses, failure on the part of a court official to properly record testimony, and on and on and on.

We feel, however, it is to our credit that we did not bow to any of this political pressure (and there was much more—including some late night telephone calls of harassment). When we started in this we told our attorney and his firm . . . we intended to follow this through and see if we did in fact still own our property or was it really owned by the State of Wisconsin as was suggested at one of the many meetings we attended during the fight.[25]

The court conceded that the case was a difficult one and that cases in other states appeared to have held such regulations unconstitutional. Not only did this not deter the judges, they even went on to enunciate a rule that could lead to wholesale expropriation of people's properties: "An owner has no absolute and unlimited right to change the essential natural character of his land so as to use it for a purpose for which it was unsuited in its natural state and which injures the rights of others."

How could this country ever have been developed had this been the law? It would not have been possible much of the time to build homes, highways, public utilities or industries. The experience of zoning in this country indicates that there are almost always some people who are or believe or contend that they are injured by new construction. Who would have wanted to invest in property confronted with the strong possibility that it would be taken away?

The land owned by the Justs is included within the conservancy district of the Marinette County shorelands zoning ordinance. This district is defined to include all shorelands designated as swamps or marshes in the United States geological survey maps, and the Justs' land is so shown. Many conclusions are contained in the opinion about the environmental significance and role of swamps and wetlands, but no evidence is cited showing the harm that would result from building on the Justs' or similarly situated property. To what extent will it pollute the lake? Will it destroy valuable ecosystems? Will it cause noxious consequences? How or to what extent will the public be damaged? The court responds to such issues with prose and not with facts. The judges are willing to uphold an exceedingly severe regulation adopted in the name of environmental protection without requiring evidence to substantiate alleged harm to the environment. On this basis, the court has failed in the fundamental judicial role of defending individual rights against the might of the state.

Individuals and corporations who seek to erect structures on wetlands are not doing so to harm the community or muddy the landscape. They have purchased land to engage in a legitimate business that presumably will serve the community. It will employ people and provide housing or other needs. Their main failing is that they have not been as successful at persuading legislators as other interests have. Legislators act in response to the pressures placed on them, and one of the most important is to please those who will maintain them in office. There is no more critical factor in the life of ambitious politicians. Courts should accordingly be dubious about and probe deeply into laws that wipe out people's investments. This is an unconscionable penalty to pay for having failed to convince the politicians.

Ironically, the penalty provision of the very ordinance in issue, by providing for a monetary forfeiture, acknowledges the great harm sustained when one's property is taken away. Many criminal laws prescribe as punishment either a monetary fine or imprisonment, or both. Imagine, however, how serious the crime would have to be before someone could be fined an amount equal to the monies lost by the Justs as a result of the court's decision.

The Just case should be viewed as one involving an individual's freedom—and possibly a nation's freedom. Cases of this nature may serve as precedents for other situations where government will decree that the common good or public interest requires elimination of other rights set forth in the constitution. That would operate to erase further the distinction between the free and the police state.

Judicial Inconsistency

The California Supreme Court, in a four to three decision, has upheld a thirty foot height limitation imposed on a large portion of the city of San Diego, as a result of a public vote.[27] This decision raises interesting questions about judicial consistency. To understand the point involved, some explanation is required of the law relating to the condemnation of property. The U.S. and all state constitutions either explicitly or implicitly, prohibit government from taking private property for public use without just compensation. These provisions are applied when a local, state or federal government condemns property, that is, forces an owner to sell his property to it for a road, highway, school, park or other "public use."

The government must compensate the owner by paying for the value of the property taken as well as for damages sustained to any part that remains. The object is to make the community, not the owner, pay the full cost of the benefit it receives.

Over the years, the courts have in many respects, enlarged the traditional law of condemnation. Compensation has even been required where there has been no actual or physical taking of property, but the owner has suffered loss as a result of certain government actions. The term "inverse condemnation" has been applied to the legal doctrine which allows such recovery. Unlike the usual condemnation action in which a sale is forced on the owner, the inverse type refers to a purchase forced on the government.

A leading case in inverse condemnation was decided by the U.S. Supreme Court in 1946. It ruled that frequent low flights by U.S. military aircraft amounted to the taking of an easement or air corridor over the property, entitling the owner to compensation.[28] Some state courts have gone further and said over-flight was not necessary; sound waves produced by aircraft could just as much reduce the use and enjoyment of the property, and the owner should likewise be awarded payment.[29]

The California Supreme Court in 1970 explained that the underlying purpose in inverse condemnation is "to distribute throughout the community the loss inflicted on the invidiudal . . . to afford relief to the landowner in cases in which it is unfair to ask him to bear a burden that should be assumed by society."[30]

That court, along with others, has also been giving the benefit of the doubt to property owners in determining the amount of compensation. In 1972, the U.S. Supreme Court, in setting a broad standard for recovery by lessees of land, reiterated that "just compensation derives as much content from the basic equitable principles of fairness, as it does from technical concepts of property law."[31]

All the while the law of condemnation has been going one way, the law of zoning has been traveling in the opposite direction. Under the theory that it constitutes regulation and is not a taking, the courts have become increasingly reluctant to overturn anything adopted in the name of zoning.

Yet zoning, by refusing to allow an owner to use land as he wishes, can similarly deprive him of huge sums. This obviously occurs when land is zoned from a more to less valuable use. While such reduction in value is one factor in zoning cases, it is not normally the decisive one. Government can, as a result, cause huge losses to owners under zoning which it could not do if the law of inverse condemnation were applied to such actions.

Consider now the case of the thirty foot height limitation. It establishes no less an easement than that created by airplanes when they fly over land, and for which compensation would be required. Nor is such a restriction of minor consequence. High-rises these days may easily be 300 to 400 feet in height and a thirty foot height regulation may therefore restrict some lands to about ten percent of potential use. The public will be benefitted in theory at least as it would if huge amounts of land were taken for parks or roads and many owners will be similarly harmed. A broad height limitation will affect many owners, both big and small, again comparable to what occurs from airplane disturbances.

Laymen reading what the judges say in inverse condemnation cases, would tend to find unbelievable the legality of the height regulation. The explanation is zoning: it stands out as a glaring exception to the protection afforded property owners by the federal and state constitutions.

Zoning and Conflicts of Interest

Some important judicial decisions concerning conflicts of interest in zoning matters have been made in recent years. If carried to their logical outcome, they could seriously curtail the zoning process that presently exists in the country.

Zoning ordinances and amendments are adopted by local legislators (councilmen, supervisors, etc.) who, it has been taken for granted, are entitled to exercise considerable discretion in making these decisions. Legislators are policy makers, and can favor causes and interests as they choose. As a general matter, courts will not even inquire into their motivations.

Legislators are, however, restricted from making decisions in instances which they have a conflict of interest, that is, where their own personal welfare will be enhanced to the point where they are willing to disregard the interests of the public. It is my view that such conflicts inevitably arise in zoning matters, since politicians have much to gain personally from voting for or against proposed development. If courts accepted such reasoning, they would be forced to curb zoning substantially. Some may be moving in that direction. Consider some recent cases.

A member of the municipal council of West Paterson, New Jersey, was a horse owner, and he voted to introduce for consideration a zoning amendment that would allow horses to be kept in a residential zone. He abstained on the vote to adopt it. His vote did not affect the outcome since the ballot both for introduction and passage was five to one. The court, however, ruled the amendment invalid, declaring that the council's action was quasi-judicial in nature, and "it is not an actual conflict of interest which is decisive, nor whether the public official succumbs to the temptation, but rather where there is a potential for conflict."[32]

In a Tacoma, Washington case, the Supreme Court of that state struck down a zoning ordinance because a member of the planning commission was employed as a loan officer by the bank that held a mortgage on the property in question. The mortgage was in default, and the rezoning would have doubled the value of the property. There was no evidence that anyone had exerted any pressure on him, or that he would personally benefit. He began negotiations for purchase of a business before the zoning hearings commenced, and bought it afterwards, leaving the employment of the bank. The vote of the planning commission to recommend rezoning was four to three, and the City Council approved unanimously.[33]

Several years previously, the Washington Court invalidated a rezoning of land which might have increased the value of nearby property owned by the chairman of the planning commission. The action of the commission was only an advisory one and passed without the need for counting the chairman's vote. The City Council had final authority and could have disregarded the commission's recommendation if it so chose.[34]

In the latter two cases, the Washington Supreme Court ruled on the basis of an "appearance of fairness doctrine" it had previously adopted. The Court explained it as follows:

Members of commissions with the role of conducting fair and impartial hearings must as far as practicable, be open-minded, objective, impartial, free of entangling influences and capable of hearing weak voices as well as the strong. . . . It is important that not only justice be done, but that it also appear to be done. . . .[35]

The Vermont Supreme Court in a case concerning a state environmental board stated that a member of it would be disqualified from acting where "his contributions or feelings generally, were significant to give him an interest in the event."[36] In a Delaware case, the state's high court disqualified the vote of the chairman of a planning board because he had acted like an "outspoken and antagonistic opponent" of the proposal and "conducted himself like an actual adversary" at a proceeding.[37]

Under the standards of these cases, many zoning determinations should fail. Quite frequently, councilmen decide cases for reasons that have nothing to do with the evidence presented to them. Their own jobs may depend on satisfying the desires of their constituents, and they cannot give equal consideration to petitioners for rezoning or to the broader interest of the community. In addition, they may, as practicing politicians, favor certain people, have made special committments in their election campaigns, or have ideological convictions concerning the issue (for example, environmentalism or pro-growth).

Some recent Watergate inspired legislation may also lend itself to restricting the zoning function. California's political reform act of 1974 contains a tough conflict-of-interest provision. The city attorney of San Diego issued an opinion that a councilman had violated this law by voting in a matter involving a project across the street from property owned by the nonprofit organization for whom he worked. This opinion was upheld by a lower court. How different is this from favoring persons or groups that will contribute money or help obtain votes on Election Day?

Some will protest these similarities, and urge courts to find a line of distinction far short of crippling zoning. Such expediency, however, would be at the expense of both the integrity and credibility of government.

Notes

1. Construction Industry Assn. of Sonoma County v. City of Petaluma, 375 F. Supp. 574 (N.D. Cal. 1974).

2. _____ F. 2d _____ (9th Cir. 1975).

3. Note: *The Right to Travel: Another Constitutional Standard for Local Land Use Regulations?* 39 U. CHI. L. R. 612 (1972).

4. Village of Belle Terre v. Boraas, 416 U.S. 1 (1974).

5. Bilbar Construction v. Board of Adjustment, 141 A.2d 851 (1958); National Land and Investment Co. v. Kohn, 215 A.2d 597 (1966); Appeal of Kit-Mar Builders, 268 A.2d 765 (1970); Appeal of Girsh, 263 A.2d 398 (1970).

6. Warth v. Seldin, 95 S. Ct. 2197 (1975).

7. Euclid v. Ambler Co., 272 U.S. 365 (1926).

8. Ybarra v. City of Town of Los Altos Hills, 503 F.2d 250 (9th Cir. 1974).

9. Cases in note 5, *supra*.

10. Board of County Supervisors v. Carper, 107 S.E. 2d 390 (1959); Board of Supervisors v. De Groff Enterprises, 198 S.E. 2d 600 (1973); Board of Supervisors v. Snell Construction Co., 202 S.E. 889 (1974).

11. Nectow v. City of Cambridge, 277 U.S. 183 (1928).

12. Seattle Title Trust Company v. Roberge, 278 U.S. 116 (1928).

13. at 390.

14. Union Oil company of California v. Morton, 512 F. 2d 743 (9th Cir. 1975).

15. REAL ESTATE RESEARCH CORP., THE COSTS OF SPRAWL (Prepared for C.E.Q., H.U.D., and E.P.A., 1974).

16. LANSING, CLIFTON AND MORGAN, NEW HOMES AND POOR PEOPLE: A STUDY OF THE CHAIN OF MOVES (Ann Arbor: U. of Mich. 1969), See discussion Chapter 2 on operation of filtering.

17. Southern Burlington County N.A.A.C.P. v. Township of Mount Laurel, 336 A.2d 713 (1975).

18. Warth v. Seldin, note 6 *supra*.

19. Southern Burlington etc., note 17 *supra*.

20. The case involved was Passack Assn. v. Mayor of Washington, 329 A.2d 89 (1974).

21. *Clinton Asked for Zoning Plan*, TRENTON N.J. TIMES-ADVERTISER, Sept. 23, 1975.

22. Note 17 *supra*.

23. Vickers v. Township Committee of Gloucester Township, 181 A.2d 129 (1962).

24. Just v. Marinette County, 201 N.W.2d 761 (1972).

25. Pennsylvania Coal Co. v. Mahon, 260 U.S. 393, 416 (1922).

26. Article by the Justs appeared in PRIVATE PROPERTY—FREE ENTERPRISE, Jan. 1974 at 10.

27. San Diego Bldg. Contractors Assn. V. City Council, 13 C.3d 205 (1974).

28. Causby v. United States, 328 U.S. 256 (1946).

29. Martin v. Port of Seattle, 391 P.2d 540 (1964); Thornburg v. Port of Portland, 376 P.2d 100 (1962); City of Jacksonville v. Schumann 167 So. 2d 95 (Fla. Dist. Ct. App. 1964).

30. Holtz v. Sup. Ct. of City and County of San Francisco, 475 P.2d 441 (1970).

31. Almota Farmers Elevator v. United States, 409 U.S. 470 (1972).

32. Netluch v. Mayor of West Paterson, 325 A.2d 517 (1974).

33. Narrowsview Preservation Assn. v. City of Tacoma, 526 P.2d 897 (1974).

34. Buell v. City of Bremerton, 495 P.2d 1358 (1972).

35. Id. at 1361.

36. In re State Aid Highway No. 1, Peru, 328 A. 2d 667 (1974).

37. Acierno v. Folsom, 337 A. 2d 309 (1975).

6

Impact of the Environmental Cause

Recreational Land and Open Space

It is often contended that this nation has not provided adequately for the physical environment of its people. But how much or what is "enough"? Contrary to this view, the record indicates that the country has in fact done quite well in this regard.

Consider what has been accomplished to preserve nature in its original state. In the belief that wilderness as such is an important natural resource, about 15 million acres of public lands are restricted to or managed for "wilderness" use. In size, that is larger than the combined total area of New Hampshire, Vermont, Delaware, and Rhode Island.

Federal law prohibits in wilderness areas the use of autos or other mechanical transport and the installation of roads or any structures. Millions of acres of productive forest land are included but timber cannot be harvested. Except largely for sections at the perimeters, the bulk of these enormously scenic territories can be enjoyed only by those physically able to walk, hike, or ride mules for very long distances, and at times crawl or cliffhang. The nation has thereby provided extravagantly for a relatively small group.

The U.S. Forest Service has been considering an additional 12 million acres in the National Forest System for possible classification as wilderness. Five million acres of our national parks have been recommended for inclusion in the wilderness system. In 1974, 800,000 acres of California's desert land were closed to any recreational vehicle use and another 10 million acres were placed under strict regulation. These controls were imposed by the Federal Bureau of Land Management in spite of vehement objections and litigation filed by recreational vehicle enthusiasts. The balance of the California desert, about 1 million acres, will remain unrestricted.

Our nation has a wide variety of recreational and open space areas and the amount keeps increasing. Here are illustrations:

1. Federal, state, and local governments continually buy land for such use. National parks now contain over 29 million acres.

From 1960 to 1970 state expenditures for parkland acquisitions quadrupled. During the seventies voters in some states authorized huge funding to buy land. Thus, California passed a $250 million bond issue for parks, beaches, and open space in 1974.

2. Private enterprise has created the Disneylands, Sea Worlds, Safaris, Busch Gardens, and a variety of recreational projects catering to millions. Users may pay an entry fee, but the public parks do not come free either. We are taxed to acquire and maintain them, and they do not pay taxes.

3. Residential developments are installing recreational facilities, and it is becoming quite common for new apartment, townhouse, and condominium developments to contain swimming pools, tennis courts, and club houses. This also occurs in single-family subdivisions. There are lush "country club" developments surrounding golf courses available to middle class groups.

4. Resorts, hotels, and motels provide recreational facilities. Some have acres upon acres devoted to golf, swimming, and tennis.

5. Civic organizations are buying land to preserve in its unaltered state. For example, Nature Conservancy, a private conservation group, recently purchased for $600,000 an 1,844 acre barrier island off Virginia's eastern shore, adding to the 7,000 acres it already owns nearby. It has been estimated that one-third of public open space in the New York metropolitan area was donated.

If still more land is needed for public use, consideration should be given to a major land owner: government. About 35 to 40 percent of the nation's land is publicly owned. Some could be privately developed for such purposes—and for the fiscal comfort of taxpayers.

The experience of Switzerland is pertinent. Hotels and restaurants have been built in mountainous areas. Railways and aerial tramways provide transportation where automobiles cannot go, allowing both the hardy and the frail to enjoy some of the world's most spectacular scenery. Nonetheless, few who have ever been to that country could possibly complain about its commitment to nature and beauty.

Buying Land to Protect the Enviromenment

The program of one national conservation organization suggests an answer to the ever-intensifying conflict between environmentalists and developers, anti and progrowthers. The group is Nature Conservancy. In 1974, it purchased for $600,000 Cobb Island, a 1,844 acre barrier island off Virginia's eastern shore.

That organization is supported by people who, according to its president, believe that direct purchase is a better way to preserve unique natural areas than depending on government regulation or purchase with the "uncertainties of politics." The conservancy already owns other barrier islands near Cobb, totalling more than 7,000 acres in size, and plans to keep all of them in a natural state and prevent development. It has purchased many other properties throughout the country, with the same objectives. A number of other organizations also engage in this practice.

Hence, instead of using their funds to fight and limit development, environmentalists can use them to purchase land for open space. They would not have to seek government coercion over others who want to use and enjoy their own property or have different interests. It is a solution most consistent with a free society. Environmental organizations are spending millions of dollars for legal and lobbying fees to influence national and local governmental policies in their direction. While some of these expenditures have accomplished their purpose, many have not. Using the same funds for purchase of properties to preserve and protect open space would clearly make every buck count, eliminating the speculative nature of their present spending policies. They would be competing in the land market, and when successful, would ensure the use of land for what they deem best. While it is hardly probable that they will succeed in Manhattan or other downtown areas, there are certainly many outlying sections where land is still reasonably priced. Many, possibly most, of these suburban and rural areas will in the future be near or in the midst of development, and, if not now, these purchases could in time serve significant environmental concerns.

Such a policy would produce much less interference in the lives of the vast majority of people who benefit from construction of homes, businesses, and industries. Environmentalists now rely largely on government regulation to accomplish land use goals, and, when effective, either may prevent the erection of a project, or, much more likely, compromise a proposed development by causing more land to be used than is necessary, that is, requiring five or ten apartments to the acre instead of fifteen or twenty, or one house, not three per acre. The additional land is still privately owned and does not become open space accessible to the public. Neither side actually benefits, and these practices are gobbling up the land. As supply decreases, its price is increased and new development sprawls needlessly further and further into the rural areas. These practices waste rather than conserve the land.

Nor does land have to be bought to control its use. By the purchase of development rights only, property can be restricted to use for single family or to partial development or to no use at all for a specified period. Developers in nonzoned areas buy such rights (in the form of restrictive covenants) to protect their projects from undesirable uses on adjoining land, and the cost is far less than that for outright purchase.

During the past ten years, had they not used the monies for legal and lobbying activities, the environmental groups could have accumulated perhaps 20 to 25 million dollars for land acquisition. Moreover, if the environmentalists had campaigned publicly on this basis for contributions, they might have received considerably more, including some from sources that strongly oppose their present policies.

Land acquisition is another private tool by which people can control the use of property. Its availability lends further support to the argument that public land use regulation is neither necessary nor desirable.

Special Interests

What are "special interests"? According to a statement issued by environmental groups, they are what caused Congress to modify existing clean air standards in the emergency energy bill that was pending prior to its recess in late 1973. This automatically categorizes as special interests a huge percentage of the American people who sought such action to conserve fuel.

Of course, those were not the special interests the environmentalists were attacking. Their targets were the coal and oil companies who were endeavoring to secure greater profits. For some it may come as a shocking disclosure, but these companies do not just consist of big tanks or great holes in the ground stockpiling thousand dollar bills. They are owned and operated by people, thousands of corporate shareholders, officials, and employees.

True, these people were seeking their own self-interest; it is doubtful, however, that they did so to any greater or lesser extent than others who favored or opposed the legislation.

Environmentalists are usually quick to respond that theirs is not a cause motivated by selfishness. Why should this make them more righteous or infallible—or less of a special interest? History is replete with examples of dedicated souls causing or fighting wars or otherwise seeking power for the sake of some ideology or religion.

Nor is it accurate to describe as selfless the practices intended to control the lives of others. Thus, environmentalists want land to remain undeveloped so they can hike and camp on it. They seek to prevent growth so they can enjoy rural surroundings. Why are these goals more noble than using the land for the production of housing or tourist accommodations?

The implication that environmentalism is a movement of the average citizen and that opposition to it comes solely from the "moneyed classes" is without basis in fact. A study in 1973 of environmental land use decision making in San Diego County, California conducted at the United States International University (USIU) suggests precisely the opposite.

According to this report, a coalition has emerged under the banner of controlled growth, which "finds its strength in the politically aware upper middle and upper class citizens of the region. Having acquired a comfortable standard of living, this segment of the population increasingly is preoccupied with 'quality of life' questions including protection of the environment in which they live."[1]

The study emphasizes that opposition to this environmental coalition is not limited to developer interests. It also comes from less affluent communities within the region, small property owners, labor leaders, and working class groups.

These conclusions are borne out by an analysis of voting in San Diego County on California's voters initiative in 1972 to restrict development along its coastline, made by James Sills of World Research, Inc. He found that the upper income areas supported the initiative and black, chicano, and blue collar precincts usually opposed it.

So it is that organized labor in California has been among the principal adversaries of the environmentalists. In the USIU survey, labor representatives rejected virtually all positions favored by leaders of environmental groups. Across the country, labor has joined with development interests to form organizations to combat the land use restrictions advocated by the environmentalists. Labor is aware that these restrictions threaten work, wages, and, therefore, *their* environment.

Bayard Rustin, long a leader in civil rights causes, summed up the difficulties poorer people face from liberal oriented environmentalists:

No doubt they have failed to consider the implications of their creed that while a no-growth economy may protect the fields and streams (which in itself is a dubious claim) it will most certainly result in untold misery for thousands of ordinary people, many of whom are the black poor of America and the poverty-stricken masses of Asia, Africa and Latin America. . . .

A few years ago the term "elitist" was often attached to those liberals who had seemingly lost touch with the values and aspirations of working people. Clearly growth's critics are guilty of defining social problems from an elitist point of view.[2]

Those living in marginal housing conditions and struggling to find and maintain jobs have other things to be worried about than the fate of the whooping crane or the caribou. There is, accordingly, a new twist in the traditional allegiances and special interests for and against collectivism. Many of the rich are seeking strict government controls allegedly to protect the environment—virtually from pre-cradle to postgrave—and many labor unions are trying to obtain a freer private market. If they are successful, these wealthy people will help bring about a socialism dedicated to furthering and enhancing the life-style of those who have achieved and are no longer seeking material success.

Environmentalist Power

Misusing Waterfront Land

The continuing efforts of elitists to impose their values and life-styles on others are potentially very harmful to the economic well being of the country. They seem determined to remake America in their own image—and that is a terrifying prospect.

Their current rage—or outrage—concerns beaches and waterfronts. They insist that these areas remain largely undeveloped. Miami Beach seems to be at the top of the hate parade: they virtually consider it a crime against nature. But if that is what Miami Beach is, then we ought to legalize crime. Development of the coastline there has been extremely beneficial to a great many Americans, and at one time to the elitists of an earlier era. Like many other beach resorts, its hotels, apartments, and condominiums have served millions well. Tourists have had an opportunity to live for short periods next to the ocean, eat in restaurants overlooking it, and swim, play, and lounge in meticulously maintained beach areas. Off-season and special group rates have allowed people of modest means to live in luxurious accommodations. Whereas its architecture may be vulgar to some, apparently it is quite acceptable to the millions who eagerly scrimp and save to enjoy it.

That is only part of the story. Thousands of people work there and were employed in the construction of the buildings and facilities. People and businesses have prospered. Federal, state, and local governments collect huge amounts of taxes. A community has developed catering to all income levels. Had present environmental pressures prevailed earlier, Miami Beach might still have been in a natural uninhabited condition, benefiting a vastly smaller percentage of the population.

Confrontations are erupting almost everywhere, it seems, over areas adjoining bodies of water, from streams to oceans, and if the elitists and environmentalists are successful, there will be an enormous misuse and waste of both the land and water.

Incredibly, Delaware's coastal zoning law prevents a group of oil companies from floating a 3,200 foot dock for supertankers in Delaware Bay, one of the best deep-water havens on the East Coast. Battles are being waged to prevent refineries, energy plants, and other developments that are best suited for location along the water from being constructed there. These projects would make life better and more comfortable for people of the states involved, and elsewhere, because no area of the country is an economic island. They would help alleviate current adverse economic conditions.

Perhaps the greatest irony of the day is provided by a development on the northern California coast known as Sea Ranch, whose future is in doubt due to that state's coastal zone act. Sea Ranch is not just another development; it has been written about and heralded throughout the world for its innovative environmental designs.

Planned to contain more than 3,000 homes, its character will be exactly the reverse of Miami Beach. It is being built in a manner consistent with its natural surroundings, around common, uniquely created open spaces. Its homes are intended to span the economic spectrum with few restrictions as to the size. About 2,000 trees have been planted, and irony of ironies, environmentalists are demanding that they be chopped down to preserve the ocean view from a highway. It is reported that the developers have invested about $30 million in the project and more than 300 homes have already been built. The concept as proposed will have to be radically altered if the local coastal authorities have their way, and if they are not overruled by the courts.

It is not as if the country is running out of nature. Contemplate these figures: About 35 to 40 percent of the total land area of this country is owned by government, and little less than 2 percent is urbanized. America is not a tropical island inhabited by partly clad natives able and willing to sustain themselves on the fruits and animals of the land and sea. It is preposterous to regulate the land as if it were.

The Trident Case

The United States is attacked and declares war. Before defense operations commence, a lawsuit is filed by environmental and anti-war groups complaining that the army, navy, and air force have not complied with the National Environmental Policy Act (NEPA) by filing an environmental impact statement (EIS). The legal action demands that no forces be dispatched until the government obeys NEPA.

However ridiculous, one cannot help considering such a possibility in view of the lawsuit filed by environmental groups to block the construction of a proposed Trident nuclear submarine base at Bangor, Washington.[3] The navy considers this base one of the most important in the nation's defense against nuclear attack. Specific authority and funding for it passed the two houses of Congress, which appropriated about $100 million dollars for initial development.

But the lawsuit in effect alleges that this does not remove the obligation of the government to file as EIS similar to what would be required if a highway, dam, or canal were contemplated. The navy did file a five-volume EIS concerning construction of the base, but the suit contends that it is defective and does not meet the requirements of the law.

Congress originally passed NEPA at the behest of environmentalists who contended that government was undertaking projects without full knowledge of their environmental consequences. This may be a seemingly noble purpose, but it is one that has given rise to a large amount of litigation because, until a court decides, there is little certainty as to what should or should not be included in the EIS and how much consideration it and its various provisions should be given.

What NEPA has clearly accomplished, however, is to give anyone who dislikes a contemplated government project an opportunity through litigation to delay or even defeat it. The list is not limited to environmentalists, as the Trident case indicates. That lawsuit was filed by two private citizens and five environmental groups, the lead one being Concerned About Trident (CAT).

What are the concerns of this organization and are they limited to the physical environment? These questions were directed at an officer of CAT by Ron Zumbrin, attorney for the Pacific Legal Foundation, a public interest law firm, that intervened in the case on the side of the government. This reply came from Philip M. Best, co-counsel of CAT:

I think Concerned about Trident is in effect an umbrella organization for people with a variety of concerns. That is, if a person feels they're concerned about it because of their concern about the weapons system as opposed to the environmental impact, some of them have been persuaded that the best route they've got for expressing that concern in a legal manner is to join in this lawsuit and determine the issue of whether those concerns are proper concerns within the ambit of NEPA.

And likewise, there are other people who may not be opposed to the nuclear submarines but may be in favor of a different configuration, and again not concerned about basing at Bangor, who likewise would be involved for the same reason.

So, it goes all the way from the gamut of those who are against war machines to those who are not concerned about the war effort, but are concerned about the environmental loan—a variety of people for a variety of reasons.

NEPA thus provides in certain situations those defeated by vote of Congress with another opportunity to scuttle legislation. A variety of groups apparently will use it to oppose various measures that would relieve the energy crunch. Efforts at oil drilling on federal off-shore properties, for example, will confront all the hurdles that NEPA has erected and, as a result, it may be many years before oil can be obtained from these sources.

The courts may rule that NEPA does not apply to defense programs or the Trident case may cause Congress to pass an exception. Otherwise, the act would give an enormous advantage to environmentalists, although environment is hardly on par with national defense. Nor, in view of the nation's energy troubles, can it possibly be in the same league as oil recovery. Legislation should not provide special interest groups with such powers over others.

NEPA was passed in the world that existed not long ago when oil was cheap and abundant and unemployment little more than a statistic. If there has to be a NEPA, it belongs to that world, not the one that confronts us today. The Trident case demonstrates the enormous problems inherent in such legislation.

Postscript. On August 22, 1975, Chief Judge George L. Hart, Jr. of the Federal District Court for the District of Columbia dismissed the suit by CAT principally on the grounds that it is not appropriate for the courts to superimpose their judgment as to Congress' and the Executive's programs affecting national security. In addition, the court found that the Navy's EIS complied with the provisions of NEPA.

Environmentalists and Energy Problems

Although battered by some recent judicial and legislative decisions, the environmental movement showed in the most recent vote on strip mining that it still packs considerable wallop. In spite of the nation's serious energy and economic troubles, the House came perilously close to overriding the president's veto.

While no one can pinpoint its precise impact, the evidence produced by the Ford administration and industry is exceedingly persuasive that the proposed legislation would operate to reduce the production of coal, drive up prices, and increase unemployment. Considering the severity of these problems, it borders on the irresponsible to take action that can exacerbate them.

Such factors do not seem to influence dedicated environmentalists, however. They usually contend that the preservation of nature's amenities are beyond the reach of numbers and dollars. In other words, that decisions affecting areas of environmental significance such as waterfront and scenic terrain cannot be made on the basis of calculation of costs and benefits because, as a recent Ford Foundation report said, such considerations "reflect only a fraction of the values that people hold dear."[4]

This approach throws out of the window any rational evaluation of the trade-offs and competing interests involved in any legislative decisions. As UCLA economics professor George Hilton has put it, "With an infinite value in the denominator, there is not much point in talking about the numerator."[5]

The environmentalists may have a point in asserting this perspective when human life is at stake. The situation is entirely different when the issue is land use.[6] Selecting undisturbed nature over development is a matter of personal choice and can scarcely be accepted as an unquestioned "good."

The notion that certain areas of the country must remain undeveloped attributes a unique and underserved importance to special values held by relatively few. Quite often there are competing uses for such property that serve mankind at least equally well. To reject the use of these lands for houses, apartments, hotels, refineries, nuclear plants, and mining would harm rather than help the physical environment and the economic and social well being of a great many. Only extraordinary and special reverence for nature, without similar deference to the condition of man, could possibly justify it.

Because this nation is dependent on a plentiful supply of energy, the environmentalists' position is bound overall to be self-defeating. For example, in the absence of production from strip mines, greater pressure would automatically accrue for the exploitation of oceanic and shale deposits. In the event environmentalists were also successful in curbing offshore drilling and shale recovery, they would have made inevitable the construction of more nuclear plants in areas that might otherwise remain undeveloped. The Naderites are ferociously battling against those plants and they would be highly disturbed with that result. If all else is stopped, we might in time have to rely on burning trees for fuel. The victories and joys of some environmentalists will lead to defeat and sorrow for others.

A comparable response can be given to the contention that

limiting recovery of certain resources will promote conservation. By postponing the production of one energy source, we accelerate development of another. Moreover, conservation by public fiat tends to be wasteful since the decision is usually made for political reasons. To force exploitation of other resources when strip mining would yield fuel at a fraction of the cost is inefficient. To require land to lie fallow when its use can satisfy human needs is a waste of that precious resource.

The strip mining battle reveals what can be expected in the coming months and years over other efforts to increase production of energy within this country. The experience of the Alaska pipeline indicates that in time most of these efforts will be defeated. That episode also reveals there will be considerable delay, much higher cost, and greater than needed dependency on foreign sources. The uncertainty of future legislative or court decisions itself appreciably inhibits investment in energy producing industries, resulting in a lesser supply.

Oil wells, heavy industry, sewer plants, and strip mining are not beautiful. Human existence often requires the ugly as well as the beautiful—particularly when the ugly performs an essential function and leads to economic tranquility. And that is beautiful.

The Threat to Development

Development vs. Preservation

Not even standing room was available in the City Council chamber of San Luis Obispo, California the night of July 21, 1975. Seventy residents spoke. No one remembered any local controversy that attracted as much attention or impassioned oratory in that small community of 30,000.

At issue was a 1,300 foot mountain, just outside the city limits. It was privately owned, and the owner, a prominent businessman in the area, was in the process of cutting a road leading to the top. Development had not otherwise touched the mountain. The owner wanted to erect in time a scenic chalet-restaurent at the peak. Thirty-seven speakers supported his efforts. The balance opposed creation of the road or any development of the mountain. One of the councilmen had introduced three resolutions intended to prevent development, and the debate concerned those proposals.

A recurrent theme of the opponents was to the effect that this was "our mountain," a rare and beautiful resource that was an inseparable part of the community. Some described the pleasures of climbing it; some displayed reverence for this "irreplaceable and majestic natural occurrence" and felt that it had been scarred by the road.

Within recent years similar controversies have occurred throughout the country as environmentalists battled attempts to develop portions of the earth they regard as environmentally "sensitive." They say that such places belong to all of the people and must remain in a natural state. Environmentalist literature has referred to private owners as tenants and caretakers serving at the pleasure of the people.

There is a totally unwarranted assumption behind such thinking. Private ownership and development does not destroy or remove land from the people. On the contrary, it is the best means to bring land to the public. In San Luis Obispo, it is more likely to be "our mountain" if developed than left untouched. Private owners are caretakers in the sense that they tend to utilize the land to its highest and best advantage and enable the maximum number of people to benefit from it.

A mountain provides beauty from two perspectives; on the ground and at its top. The view from the peak is usually more overwhelming than the one from the valley. If a mountain remains undeveloped, only rugged climbers will have the opportunity to enjoy most of the magnificence it offers. A chalet-restaurant will enable many more thousands to enjoy the beauty of nature.

It will also provide a host of economic benefits. These include livelihoods for those who build and later work for it, increased revenues for other businesses that will directly or indirectly serve the development and its employees, and more real estate and sales tax receipts. This nation is hardly in an economic position to stifle business activity, and the experience of New York City indicates dire prospects for cities that ignore the primacy of financial considerations.

For the most dedicated environmentalists, anything man-made on that mountain will desecrate it. That feeling borders on the religious: a special reverence for nature. Perhaps government has no more obligation to support it than any other faith, for there must be separation of religion and state under our constitution. That faith is, however, amply provided for in this nation. Close to 98 percent of our land remains unurbanized and over 15 million acres, including some of the most spectacular terrain in the world, are designated by federal law as wilderness areas. The law prohibits all roads and development in these areas, thereby providing most generously for the heartiest nature lovers.

Little is more subjective than the perception of beauty. The mountain in question, one of a chain leading to the ocean, is not particularly distinguished and would scarcely elicit special attention except from local residents for whom it represents the view from the window or yard. The new road threading its way to the top is like so many other access roads on mountains everywhere in that it, too, is unnoticed by all except those who have special concern.

Elected bodies are unsuited to make judgments about aesthetics. They supposedly represent a majority and there is no relationship between numbers and beauty. Land use controls allow political majorities to suffocate individualism in beauty and creativity, qualities upon which the progress of our civilization is dependent.

Many who now condemn development would not have been there except for development. The condition of man was greatly enhanced as nature succumbed to the designs of builders. In many areas, man's efforts created considerable beauty. Marshes were drained and trees and foliage planted. Houses, buildings, stores, and factories were erected to satisfy human needs. All became "ours" upon completion.

Controversy at the World Fair

How can a city rid itself of a dilapidated, unsightly section in or near downtown? The answer given in Spokane, Washington was to construct a world's fair in that area and replace the blight with new structures, parks, and open space. Not only would the area be transformed, but the city's economy would boom.

In some portions of the country, antigrowth forces by making that sort of approach politically unwise, have stifled building and development of their communities. Not so in Spokane. Its citizens wanted and obtained a fair to promote growth.

Businessmen in that city of about 250,000 underwrote loans from local banks and sponsored a $5 million bond issue. Railroads contributed without charge property they owned in the area. Additional development funds came from specially levied business and occupation taxes and (of course) the federal government (about $4.5 million). The fair did not break even but all losses were paid out of funds pledged by businessmen.

Local economic studies indicate that the fair created thousands of new jobs in the Spokane area and pumped many millions directly into the city's economy. Officials estimated that there would be additional millions in expenditures in Spokane and Washington State as a result of the fair. And the lives of a lot of people were made more desirable, pleasurable, and comfortable. That should be the major message of the fair.

A far different gospel, however, was preached at the United States pavilion, the largest sponsored by the eleven participating nations. It cost the United States taxpayers more than $11.5 million and its main theme was hardly representative of their attitudes and feelings. Although the exhibit was directed by the Commerce Department, the government's environmentalists took over and sold their one-sided wares under the banner, "The Earth does not belong to man; man belongs to the Earth."

These words are attributed to an Indian chief of more than a century ago. While it may have been appropriate to his culture, fortunately this country has so far given it little credence. It is a philosophy of stagnation. The present generation is deeply indebted to prior ones for not having practiced it. If the land had not been cleared, and the waters harnessed, ours would have remained a primitive society. Had less been created on and from the land over the years, our standard of living would have been correspondingly lower.

That theme has another disquieting note. Its implications are essentially totalitarian since it would require for fulfillment state coercion over the individual. Most people want to use nature to elevate their condition in life, and only the most powerful of government controls can prevent them from doing so. Well aware of this, the environmentalist movement is continually seeking new and stronger laws over human action.

The exhibits in the American pavilion failed to explain the huge burden of environmental regulation to individual freedom and to the country's economy and progress. These were most regretable omissions, totally inconsistent with the obligations of government to give an objective, truthful presentation of controversial issues. Government agencies are supposed to serve us, not direct our thinking.

Most of the exhibits on display at the fair indicated how man's conquest of the elements has led to a better life. They did not explain, however, that this could not have occurred if the progress of society had been frozen in the past by the highly exaggerated ecological threats and fears that permeated other exhibits. Humans should have demanded equal time.

Modern Soothsayers

It is exceedingly hazardous to decide current policy on speculations about the distant future. We already encounter enough difficulty simply trying to understand the here and now.

Although these observations may appear self-evident, many apparently disagree. They urge the adoption of restrictive laws over human conduct on the basis of their predictions of the future. Two things are particularly disturbing: First, the advocacy of certain environmental and conservation measures for the sake of "generations yet unborn." Second, forecasts of what materials and resources will be available to future generations.

In the absence of special occult powers, it is rather foolish to describe the wants and desires of people who still have not arrived on this earth, "the generations yet unborn." How many parents can know the course any of their children, whom they observe daily, will follow?

Such forecasting is usually part of some discussion pushing severer environmental regulations, and the world these writers and speakers contend the unborn will want usually is no different from the one they seek for themselves. What it amounts to essentially, is that they are talking about only their own desires and preferences, not anyone else's. Of course, our children should inherit the best of all possible worlds, and it should include clean air and water, beaches, parks, open space, scenic areas. But it should also be one of good living and economic conditions; jobs, desirable housing conditions and fewer slums, among other things.

Tomorrow's children will be stronger in body and mind if the economic circumstances of their parents and grandparents are satisfactory. The world they inherit also will be infinitely superior if it is a freer one, without government coercions stifling its citizens' aspirations. Accordingly, these discussions of the future are really about the present, the needs and priorities of our society.

Similarly many writers are mixing in much of their own feelings and inclinations when they demand strong conservation controls over our resources to prevent depletions in the future. These people frequently are hostile to technology and materialism. They tend to ignore the problems that would be created for those having a different perspective.

It is impossible to foretell the future on the basis of what exists today. The story of Reverend Thomas Malthus needs frequent retelling. He was a prominent British economist and sociologist, who predicted in 1798 that the food supply would not keep pace with population growth, and consequently the world was doomed to widespread starvation, poverty and distress.

Although his analysis seemed plausible in light of the information then available, his fundamental error was in making a prediction on that subject. No matter how wise he was, he could not have envisioned that man would be so resourceful that a time would come when a government would pay farmers billions of dollars not to grow crops.

We enjoy vastly more material comforts than our great grandparents did because of human skill, ingenuity and creativity. The basic resources of the world have dwindled since then, but the knowledge and understanding of how to obtain, amplify and substitute for them has increased enormously. So long as incentives exist, man's wisdom will operate to create the new and improve the old.

Historical experience discloses that substitutes or new products normally replace essential materials and resources as they become scarcer, and that when necessary, man will adjust reasonably well to a reduction in the supply of particular items. To live a life of self-sacrifice based on other premises is an abuse of a precious organism: man. Who not very long ago would have conceived of antibiotics, space travel, atomic energy, synthetic fabrics, plastics, TV, computers, lasers, jet propulsion?

To accommodate the modern soothsayers requires considerable inconvenience and hardship, especially on the part of the less affluent who depend for a better life on more production and growth.

Soothsayers preaching such human sacrifice should lose their licenses.

The Benefits of Growth

Over the years in this country, there has been substantial improvement in the living conditions of the average citizen. Those in the lower and middle classes have been receiving steadily more money to spend and have been able to enjoy an increasing standard of living. These gains are attributable to the growth in the nation's production of goods and services. Growth, consequently, must not be discouraged by government at any level if this trend is to continue and be augmented.

Greater production leads to better living conditions for two reasons. First, it will result in the employment of larger numbers of people, and that of course means bigger incomes for more persons. Wages and salaries will rise as the percentage of employed people increases. Second, the more things created and in existence, the larger the probability that everyone, from top to bottom in the income scale, will own one of these things. For example, if over a time period, twenty million autos are manufactured, it is much more likely that someone of average or less income will own one than would occur if half that number had been built. The more there are, the lower will be the cost of each, and in time new cars will filter down from rich to poor.

There is relatively little disagreement among economists as to the success of growth in raising living standards. In his book, published in 1958, *The Affluent Society,* liberal economist John Kenneth Galbraith states: "It is the increase in output in recent decades, not the redistribution of income, which has brought the great material increase, the well-being of the average man."[7]

Statistics in Galbraith's book show the large rise in income among people in the middle and lower income brackets during and following World War II. Between 1941 and 1950, the lowest fifth in income of all families increased their income by 42 percent (after income taxes); for the next to the lowest fifth, the increase was 37 percent, and for the middle fifth, 24 percent. With the notable exception of the top 5 percent, family earnings rose markedly. The earnings of the upper 5 percent declined by 2 percent. (These figures as well as others reported in this essay are adjusted to reflect changes over the years in the value of money.)

Galbraith notes that increasing aggregate output has the practical effect of reducing inequality between income groups, and thereby eliminating the more acute tensions associated with inequality. He says: "As the rich have become more numerous, they have inevitably become a debased currency."

Henry Hazlitt, a conservative economist, updates Galbraith's figures in a 1973 book entitled, *The Conquest of Poverty*.[8] He reports that the median income of families in this country (measured in 1969 prices) was $4,779 in 1949, $6,808 in 1959 and $9,433 in 1969. From the period 1939 to 1969, disposable, after-tax income (at 1958 prices) more than doubled from $1,190 to $2,517 per capita. Average gross weekly earnings (in terms of 1967 prices) rose from $56.83 in 1939 to $117.95 in 1969.

People have also been able to prosper in terms of the conveniences they have. Common people have amenities that once were reserved exclusively for the wealthy. Hazlitt cites government figures showing that in 1969, of those households with annual incomes below $3,000, 44 percent owned cars; 77 percent owned TV sets and 75 percent owned refrigerators or freezers. For those with incomes between $3,000 and $4,000, the percentages were: 67 percent owned cars; 83 percent, TV's and 76 percent refrigerators or freezers. These findings are quite remarkable considering that in 1969 government statisticians placed the "poverty theshhold" at $3,721 for a family of four, and $4,386 for a family of five.

Growth is not without its problems, however, and those opposed try hard to find them. It is said that great material accomplishments have not made people more happy and contented.

This may be true for the wealthy. For those who already own five cars and six homes, the opportunity to purchase another is hardly inspirational. That is clearly not the situation of those without either, who have to rely on growth to obtain them. Can anyone seriously suggest that the recession made people happy and contented? No-growthers contend that growth causes pollution problems and wastes the world's resources. The experience of the current recession clearly shows, however, that we have much more to fear from pursuing non-growth programs.

Notes

1. TIRADO, FELDMAN, and BECERRA, REGIONAL ENVIRONMENTAL MANAGEMENT IN SAN DIEGO COUNTY: A STUDY OF ENVIRONMENTAL LAND USE DECISION-MAKING, Chap. III, (United States International University, 1973).

2. Rustin, *No-Growth and the Poor,* SAN DIEGO EVENING TRIBUNE July 31, 1975.

3. Concerned About Trident v. Schlesinger, Fed. Dist. Ct. Dist. of Columbia, No. 74-1184.

4. A TIME TO CHOOSE AMERICA'S ENERGY FUTURE, Final Report of the Ford Foundation Energy Policy Project (1975).

5. Hilton, *A Time to Choose As Economic Thought* in NO TIME TO CONFUSE, A CRITIQUE OF THE FINAL REPORT OF THE ENERGY POLICY PROJECT OF THE FORD FOUNDATION, 105 (San Francisco: Institute for Contemporary Studies, 1975).

6. Some lands are subject to adverse soil and water conditions that may make ordinary construction a hazardous undertaking. Such problems can be controlled through building or subdivision ordinances and do not require the adoption of land use regulations. See Appeal of Kit-Mar Builders, 268 A.2d 765(1970).

7. GALBRAITH, THE AFFLUENT SOCIETY, 96 (Boston: Houghton Miflin Company, 1958).

8. HAZLETT, THE CONQUEST OF POVERTY (New Rochelle, N.Y: Arlington House, 1973).

7

The Effect of Private Market Forces

Understanding the Market

Oregon has been trying for many years to stop growing. Instead, it was in 1974 growing twice as fast as its neighbor to the south, California, and three times faster than Washington, its neighbor to the north. That experience should tell us something about how difficult it is to control human conduct. But it makes little impact in today's lecture and literary circuits where cures are continually being prescribed for those ills of the cities that exist only in the minds of the speakers and the writers.

As problem-prone as cities are, it can at least be said that most of their privately owned developments do bear relationship to what the people who live in them want. This would never be the case if these critics had their way. They fail to understand that builders do build for people and, if they engaged in that task, the critics would only be building for themselves.

Consider the new town of Reston, Virginia: Leading architects and planners were given almost complete discretion to plan and design it and their results were widely heralded by writers and commentators. It was a major effort to produce a new type and character of city by professionals highly schooled in architecture, urban design, and planning. There was only one thing wrong— people did not like it or could not afford it, and the houses did not sell well. Reston's founder was removed from control and replaced by a corporation willing to listen to the market. It then became highly successful.

To succeed, businessmen have to learn to produce what people want. Very often the quality and aesthetics of their products are rejected by the so-called "taste makers," but this is inevitable since they are building usually for a market whose capacities and tastes are totally different from and largely incomprehensible to these critics.

They must build with inexpensive materials and avoid expensive "aesthetics" when the market is incapable of accepting costly accommodations. Of what value is it to build an apartment that will have to rent for $500 a month if no one is available to rent it?

To meet the standards of the would-be taste makers would probably assure some form of financial distress or bankruptcy, for these standards generally are not consistent with the basic need to achieve maximum consumer acceptance. The critics' tastes can be satisfied when and only when they are representative of the people for whom the product is being created.

Many ordinary and not especially accomplished individuals have achieved success in business because they operate in a manner that I liken to "souped up" automobile engines, thereby maximizing whatever abilities they have. Virtually all their energies and time are dedicated and devoted to achieving success—which essentially means trying to achieve a profit by satisfying consumers.

An individual who diligently devotes twelve to fifteen hours a day to solving a problem is likely to have greater success at it than one who spends only a fraction of that time, almost regardless of who has more brains or education. Similar incentives are certainly not available to the critics or to government officials or planners, who tend to follow nine to five regimes, not risking their livelihoods upon failure and not receiving the proverbial pot of gold for success.

Such highly motivated persons have enormous contributions to make to society provided they are allowed freedom to create, innovate, and compete and are not stifled by government.

Competition: Key to Consumer Dominance

In 1973 rezoning to permit the construction of a major regional shopping center was requested for a large tract of land located in a northern portion of San Diego. People were upset, and the usual maneuvering and protesting took place. Some local officials expressed opposition because the new shopping center, by creating additional competition, would diminish the profits of existing businesses within the city. It was even suggested that merchants make a mass protest against the proposed center.

There is no doubt that the more business facilities in existence, the greater the competition each will confront. But this is about the worst reason in a private enterprise society to deny anyone access to the market. We live in a society that is highly dependent upon competition. We rely upon competition to protect the consumer and stimulate the introduction of new, more, and better products and services. There is no governmental agency available to accomplish these vital tasks; nor can government benefit the consumer and society even remotely as well, as any traveler to the socialist countries can confirm. The consumer is king when competition abounds; he is a serf when it is controlled and restricted.

A new shopping center will have to provide something better or different to attract customers—and the older centers may have to change their methods and improve products and services to keep pace. For consumers, the result will be some or many lower prices and larger varieties and better selections. Life will be made that much easier and more comfortable for many people.

The concept of open competition is innate to this country as evidenced by the antitrust laws that are intended to make the deliberate elimination of competition a crime. If, for instance, several builders within a city were to agree to build a certain number of apartment buildings and to prevent any others from being built, laws would quickly be adopted, if they did not exist, to dissolve this agreement and possibly even penalize the parties involved. This is because such an agreement would give the initiators special economic powers. Zoning accomplishes the same result when it limits construction or development. The owners of existing buildings would in either situation be able to charge higher rents and/or offer poorer services and/or avoid undertaking improvements and rehabilitation.

Might there be too much or "cut-throat" competition so that we need zoning to save us from such a fate? The answer is that there can never be too much competition from the consumer's vantage point—and everyone is a consumer. Businessmen who voluntarily enter a market should bear the risk of competition; they can take into account this risk when they commit their funds. Moreover, why should those who are part of the market be given preferred status over those who want to enter it?

Nor is is it possible for anyone to determine the "correct" amount of business competition. There are always many uncertainties in the business world and it is difficult to evaluate precisely market conditions pertinent to any proposed development. Future economic and population trends are exceedingly difficult to project accurately for any one area, and this is compounded by changes in demand caused by the shifting desires and needs of people, all of which may glut or unglut a market. This is a risk that can much better be borne by entrepreneurs rather than consumers.

Considering something such as the proposed shopping center, the self-interest of existing businesses would dictate opposition to any additional competition. Unfortunately, such self-interest has often been a major factor in zoning decisions; businessmen have frequently used overt or covert influence to try to kill proposed rezoning that would create more competition. Would-be developers can also be expected to exert similar efforts and, regrettably, the outcome of the competition for the favor of the local politicians may determine whether development will occur.

Some contend that this state of affairs must be tolerated because zoning regulations will, in the long run, provide for better quality, both materially and environmentally. What such a stand fails to comprehend are the benefits achieved by society whenever new development occurs.

Owners do not use their property in a vacuum. They have to make a product that someone will want to buy. It may be a new, different or improved item, or quite often, a lower price. Possibly the greatest beneficiaries of competition are those who own little or no property. The developers of the fast food franchises and coin operated washing and dry cleaning machines have benefitted enormously people of lower incomes, probably more so than a host of charitable or government programs. Examples abound everywhere in our society. Literally millions of people using their time, energy and ingenuity in their own interest are thereby creating better living opportunities for others as well as for themselves.

Not all businessmen reap the profit they seek, but once they have produced goods in quest of that profit, supply has been increased and that always benefits the consumer. Furthermore, as production occurs there is an increase in business activity and employment both of which add to people's earnings.

Problems do occur and the process is far from perfect. The best remedy against a poor product is the opportunity for someone else to create a better one. Good products drive out bad ones. Zoning regulations limit entry into the market and prevent that from occurring , thereby insulating poor performance from competition.

The competitive process has led to the very high standards of living in this country. To restrict it is to retard substantially the progress and well-being of our society.

Development Patterns

Coping With Growth

Cities and towns do not come packaged in boxes like erector sets. Cities are arising in the West near new mining operations, and newspaper and TV reporters seem disturbed that housing, schools, and shopping facilities are not standing in these desolate areas waiting for people to arrive. They keep interviewing the new inhabitants who say what most should be expected to say, that conditions are not very pleasant.

But how can it be otherwise? Anyone who would have demanded the creation of housing in these areas several years ago, before the energy and resources crisis made such areas economically important, might have been committed. On the other hand, if mining and production are delayed until all workers are comfortably ensconced in their respective dream homes, the resources will not be mined for years to come—if ever. The workers would suffer along with the rest of us.

It is inevitable that boom towns bring living problems for those attracted by the prospect of new riches and lush jobs. This was the story of the American West, now probably the best housed portion of the country. The settlers usually anticipated the kinds of hardship they found, but chose them in preference to the life they left behind in the East. They developed great portions of the country and succeeding generations were well served.

The best to be hoped for in these situations is that the developers and builders will be allowed to respond to the demand for housing and shopping, and not be hamstrung by zoning and building regulations. Schools and other facilities will follow.

This course of action, however, can bring added fury from the press. They may charge that the builders and speculators are desecrating the landscape, selecting sites that are scenic attractions or perhaps the habitat of unique four-legged creatures. And it may well be true of some of these potential sites. However, the buildings will have to go somewhere. If new construction is required to bypass the challenged areas, houses will be located longer distances from shopping and employment. And the arguments about how the land should be used will delay considerably new construction.

The usual way out of this dilemma is to demand planning and regulation, and then more and more of the same when the prior doses do not work. That is today's automatic cure-all for those who keep insisting on perfect solutions to these problems. Greater and greater powers will then be given to politicians, bureaucrats, and planners, hardly a winning combination. But regardless of their knowledge or wisdom, they will be unable to accomplish the politically or physically impossible—yet, that is what will be demanded of them.

Thus, to obtain more housing on less land requires taller structures. The mere mention of this, however, tends to evoke deletable expletives from environmentalists and planners. They prefer bigger lots to provide more open space, but want them to cost less and take up less land. They would like more housing but less construction. The regulatory process invariably curtails development. Fewer housing units will be created and there will be additional horrors to report.

A more realistic and responsible approach to these difficulties is required. While new growth may create problems for people, the history of new development in this country shows that most of them will be solved within a few years. I doubt that conditions in life were idyllic where these people previously lived—else why did they migrate? When individuals move they usually do so to better themselves.

The more we allow normal market processes to operate unhampered, the quicker the solutions will arrive.

Traditional Development Patterns

At a zoning hearing some years ago, a commissioner expressed opposition to a proposed major apartment complex because there were not enough churches in the area. I replied that if people wanted them, they would in time be built. Who, I asked, can be expected to build churches on speculation?

The issue thus presented is a very lively one today. Should development be allowed in areas where the roads, schools, shopping centers, sewer, water, and other facilities are not adequate to service an increased population? Many communities are seeking to answer the question in the negative, and are accordingly adopting highly restrictive zoning ordinances limiting construction. Although on the surface this policy must seem advantageous to potential buyers, actually it is not. On the contrary, it can be extremely harmful to the great mass of housing consumers.

The traditional pattern of development in this country is that except for sewer and water facilities, houses and people arrive first, followed in time by new or enlarged roads, schools, shopping facilities, churches, hospitals, etc. While initial residents may sustain discomforts, within a few years the missing services will usually have been amply provided.

This has been the story of development in this country, and it cannot be otherwise. There would have been considerably less expansion if builders were required to wait for roads and schools to be built or enlarged. Nor can taxpayers be expected to undertake such large expenditures when future development is only a possibility. Who can predict with any degree of certainty where, when, and how rapidly construction will occur? Can you imagine building a new school and letting it sit unoccupied waiting for students to move into an area? Much the same can be said about installation of major roads, shopping centers, churches, and hospitals.

The situation is not similar regarding water and sewer service. Buildings are not liveable unless these services are available for use. This is a matter of health and sanitation or municipal service regulations. It should be added that zoning controls tend to confuse the issue because they concern many other matters. As a matter of fairness, every piece of property should have the same opportunity as any other to obtain these services.

Should we allow people to live in an area where the schools, roads, and other facilities are still inadequate? The answer is clearly yes, because people should have the choice of deciding between these inadequacies and others that undoubtedly exist where they presently live. They are not being compelled to rent or buy in a new area.

Most people do not live under optimum living conditions; they must instead select the best for themselves from that which is available, and this process involves highly personal and private decisions. Millions of people live in accommodations not ideal by many standards and would like to improve their surroundings in at least some, if not most, respects. Countless numbers have voluntarily selected to pay relatively high prices and rents to live in housing that many others find objectionable. An obvious example is presented by the many apartment buildings contiguous to railroad tracks, expressways, industrial developments, gas stations, and below or close to airplane flight paths. Tenants have chosen to live in these buildings and accept the noise, dirt, and other unpleasantnesses rather than live in other buildings that they apparently believe have greater disadvantages. Perhaps the buildings they have selected are located closer to their work, near better transportation, or offer cheaper rents or better facilities.

There is an area in San Diego known as Mira Mesa, where major development began in 1969 and the conditions of the schools there are still less desirable than elsewhere in the area. The press and TV continually draw attention to this problem, so few buyers can be said to be unaware of it. Yet, Mira Mesa has rapidly developed and prices continue steadily upward. Apparently purchasers there have concluded that the homes are still a good buy in spite of the difficulties with schools, a situation that, however, might deter others.

Reasons for moving vary, but seem consistent in at least one respect: When people move it is likely that they are bettering themselves. It should be a fundamental purpose of government to encourage this process.

Are buyers often misled or denied sufficient information? Very little, in my experience. They can easily make comparisons with what they presently have. There is even less likelihood of this occurring when competition exists and one seller can criticize another's product. Those concerned with this problem consequently should encourage more competition. Further, most buyers and builders require substantial long-term mortgage financing of twenty-five or so years, and the mortgage lenders or guarantors should be most knowledgeable and concerned about the quality of the housing in which their money is invested for so lengthy a period.

Communities that require facilities to be in existence or installed before they allow construction in an area will necessarily have to stop much proposed construction, reducing the production of housing and thereby raising its price. If there are any benefits to be derived from such a policy by existing residents, and this is highly questionable, it is more than offset by the detriments suffered by those who seek better housing. They are either denied any or a variety of choices—and that is contrary to the objectives of any rational economic system.

Laws that limit production generally have that same effect on people's opportunities to better their conditions in life.

Toward Private Planning

Houston has never adopted zoning, but it has imposed a limited number of land use regulations, far fewer than exist in any zoned community. The number and importance of these regulations has increased over the years, but not appreciably. In contrast, the other major cities have been steadily enlarging the number and severity of their land use controls. Although the land use system popularly engaged in has always been referred to as "zoning", there is little similarity between the regulations instituted at the advent of zoning and those now operative.

In effect, a number of zoning institutions have come and gone. As zoning was originally envisioned, the local authorities were to adopt detailed regulations that would allow or cause development to occur automatically, and without the need to exercise official discretion except to grant relief in relatively few instances. The system that now prevails is nearly the reverse of that. Discretion predominates, and permits for development are granted or withheld quite frequently on the basis of whether the councilmen approve of what is proposed.

Cities are continually amending their zoning ordinances, either in large or small measure. Experience has shown this to be a never-ending process. The plan that was "perfect," the solution that was "ideal," and the settlement that was "satisfactory" frequently turn out in practice to be anything but. When the ones on the books do not work or prove undesirable to the politically powerful, new plans and laws have to be created and success is no more likely than before.

The constantly changing laws suggest that citizens have been no more satisfied with any other version than they were with the original. In Houston, on the other hand, the evidence is that residents have maintained confidence in nonzoning. In both 1948 and 1962, Houston voters rejected zoning in straw votes, and an event that occurred in July 1975 indicates that this sentiment has not changed.

A zoning issue arose at that time in connection with a proposed application by Houston for a grant of $100,500 from the U.S. Department of Housing and Urban Development (HUD). The money was to be used for a comprehensive planning study for future growth, possibly a requirement for obtaining funds from HUD in the future. It sounded like zoning to some, and the mayor, to allay such fears, caused a stipulation to be placed in the proposed ordinance stating: "None of these funds shall be used to study or recommend zoning." City planners assured the council that the contemplated study would avoid the zoning issue and there was no need for concern.

All of this still did not satisfy a majority of the city council, which, by a five to three vote, defeated the ordinance, principally on the grounds that the federal grant might be the first step toward zoning. Those voting in favor of the application to HUD should not be considered necessarily as zoning supporters. The mayor voted for it but he has gone on record against the adoption of zoning. He has written that the "economic and social profile of Houston is such that traditional approaches such as zoning and land use controls are unneeded and undesirable."

Readers of zoning literature ought to ponder the Houston situation as they digest the millions of words that are written annually in the cause of greater zoning regulation. It exists successfully in spite of all the warnings of catastrophe that many zoning writers forecast for municipalities that do not minutely plan and regulate land use.

Houston in July 1975 had one of the strongest economies of any city in the nation. The Council on Municipal Performance, a New York based organization, rated Houston and Indianapolis as the cities with the healthiest economies in 1974. Nonzoning did not create Houston's boom, but it has contributed mightily to it by allowing expansion without the inevitable restraints of the political process. There are relatively few obstacles imposed by that community on the initiative, imagination and creativity of those who build and develop cities. These are the producers of our society that public planning and political considerations inevitably hold back. Governmental planning disturbs, impedes and often ruins private planning.

In some cases localities make deliberate efforts to curb development. But even where this is not the objective, the planners, politicians and citizens that control zoning are incapable of creating rules that do not stifle production and development. Much of our cities are zoned to permit those buildings which no developer in his right mind would consider, and to forbid the kind of construction which the market eagerly seeks. Public planning involves regulating the future on the basis of the past or present, and this eliminates the flexibility needed to cope with the new, the unexpected and the innovative.

Probably most Americans would instinctively understand and accept this analysis. They would readily concur in the premise that this country is founded on individual action and initiative, and oppose the granting of huge powers to government officials. This has occurred in zoning, and it is as wrong there as it would be elsewhere in society.

Index

143

About the Author

Bernard H. Siegan is Distinguished Professor of Law at the University of San Diego School of Law. He teaches courses in land use and law-and-economics. He writes a weekly column that appears in various newspapers across the country.

Mr. Siegan is by profession a lawyer, having graduated with a J.D. degree from the University of Chicago Law School in 1949. He was admitted to practice before the Illinois and Federal courts in 1950. He was a practicing attorney in Chicago, specializing in real estate law until moving in June 1973 to La Jolla, California, where he now resides. In Chicago he was also an investor in companies that owned and developed real estate.

During the 1968-69 school year, Siegan was Research Fellow in Law and Economics at the University of Chicago Law School. He is the author of the book, LAND USE WITHOUT ZONING (1972, Lexington Books), and has written many articles on land use, and urban planning and zoning, which have been published in professional journals, magazines, and newspapers.